FOREVER SPRING

ALYCE ZULKOSKI

Recollections of bygone days,
yet forever a memory!

Scripture quotations from The New American Bible,
Saint Joseph Edition

Copy of the poem "The Swing" by Robert Lewis Stevenson

Copy of the poem "My Shadow" by Robert Lewis Stevenson

Excerpts from Elson-Gray Basic Readers, Teacher's Guide
Pre-Primer and Primer

Author's Note: Some who read this may have a different recollection
of some events, however; these are my memories.
This is the way I remember them. At no time has there been an attempt
to defame or mislead anyone.

Cover Design and Book Design by Alyce Zulkoski and Andrea J. Moreau
Cover depicts Alyce and Gary walking to school, mom and dad on their wedding day.
The Valentine dates back to 1912, a gift to mom from her grade school friend.

Edited by:
Ann Milton and Keith Blackledge

Library of Congress Control Number 2003094920

ISBN 09729670-0-1

Published by Spectrum Quick Copy Center
North Platte, NE 69101

First Printing, 2003
Additional copies may be attained by writing to the author,
Alyce Zulkoski, 1307 Burlington, North Platte, NE 69101-5730
E-Mail: Alyceaz@nponline.net

See order form in back of book

Dedication

To my parents,
my first
and best role models

Casimir James Zulkoski
Born--March 13, 1902
Died--April 15, 1981

Anna Catherine Valasek Zulkoski
Born--July 4, 1904
Died--April 28, 1998

ACKNOWLEDGEMENTS

I wish to thank the members of the *Old 101 Writers Group* for their encouragement and support as my book began to take form.

To Ann Milton, a published author for her special interest, wise council as I proceeded with the various aspects of publishing my book.

To Keith Blackledge, the self described "Old Editor' of the North Platte Telegraph with red ink in hand, beautifully edited the manuscript.

To Andrea Moreau, for her enthusiastic approach to developing the format and bringing the book into reality. Together, we designed a memorable cover, capturing the essence of the story-line.

To all the people mentioned in the book, some no longer with us, but whose lives touched mine as I journeyed to adulthood.

And lastly, though very importantly, *to my brother Gary* who shared my journey, creating memorable moments, and cherished memories as they became the heart of this book.

The Practice of Virtues
Colossians, 3:12-15

Because you are God's chosen ones, holy and
beloved, clothe yourselves with heartfelt mercy, with
kindness, humility, meekness, and patience.

Bear with one another. Forgive whatever grievances
you have against one another. Forgive as the Lord
has forgiven you.

Over all these virtues put on love
which binds the rest together and makes them
perfect. Christ's peace must reign in your hearts,
since as members of the one body you have been
called to that peace.

Authors Note:
This passage was read at mom's wake
by Father Bernard Berger, Pastor
St. Mary's Catholic
Church in Sargent Nebraska.

In life and even in death,
mom yearned for peace.

FOREWORD

It has been a long-time dream of mine to document the early growing up days of my brother and myself. The intent isn't so much focused on us but rather on how it was living as family with our father Casimir (Casper) and our mother Anna. They grew up before the great depression, in very poor, hard times. Their marriage was February 15, 1928 at the Assumption of the Blessed Virgin Mary Catholic Church in Sargent, just as the country was moving into the depression.

Dad's parents, Peter and Anna (Michalski) Zulkoski and nine children lived on a farm west of Sargent.

Tragedy struck in January 17, 1918 when his mother and two brothers, Anthony and Floyd were fatally burned in an early morning fire in their small frame house.

Mom's parents, Frank and Emma (Ptacnik) Valasek lived on a small farm north of Comstock. Her father died of throat cancer at an early age, around forty, leaving her mother to raise six children.

Dad and mom began their married life on an acreage in Valley County, north of the Bohemian Hall. Life was hard, possessions were few. My brother, Gerald and I were born in Valley County, at home with the help of Dr. Kirby McGrew, nurse Shirley Pearl and grandma Emma Valasek. They moved to a country home in

Custer County while I was just an infant. The farm was owned by grandma Valasek and would in later years be purchased by my parents. I believe the purchase price was around $6000. Dad had great difficulty making payments of $26.00 a month. It is located five miles north of Comstock. At that time there was a small square house, the common style in those early years. A barn with hayloft sat on a rise just north of the house. Living was very simple out of necessity. No electricity, no indoor plumbing or bathroom, no central heat. Income was dependent on meager harvests of corn or grain and the sale of milk, cream and eggs to the local merchants and the sale of cattle and hogs.

As I reflect on those early meager years and the luxurious living most of us experience today, it seems almost surreal, like a dream. I am grateful to have lived through and experienced that time in history in my life. It does seem unreal that so many changes could have happened in my lifetime. It is therefore, the reason for attempting to recapture a bit of that history. It seems somehow fitting to recall those hard times, relating how a devoted couple overcame the adversities and together worked, scrimped and saved until they gradually could enjoy a comfortable life with some of the luxuries the world had to offer in later years. I am hopeful that my daughter, her children and my brother and his children can read it, reflect on their heritage with renewed respect for their grandparents and in some small way find a special joy and contentment in knowing the heritage that is theirs.

The lesson of course is that we can all overcome adversities. We can all succeed with honest, hard work, caring for and sharing with one another. Intertwined in a successful life is a firm faith foundation. It is the only way one can truly measure life a success. We can all waver, we can all err in judgments but in the end, we know that there is unconditional forgiveness. My favorite biblical reading is a portion of the Last Judgment. It outlines for each of us what life on this earth is about, seeing the Lord in each other.

Matthew 25: 34-40.

The king will say to those on his right: 'Come. You have my Father's blessing! Inherit the kingdom prepared for you from the creation of the world. For I was hungry and you gave me food, I was thirsty and you gave me drink., I was a stranger and you welcomed me, naked and you clothed me. I was ill and you comforted me, in prison and you came to visit me.' Then the just will ask him: 'Lord, when did we see you hungry and feed you or see you thirsty and give you drink? When did we welcome you away from home or clothe you in your nakedness? When did we visit you when you were ill or in prison? The king will answer them: 'I assure you, as often as you did it for one of the least of my brothers, you did it for me.'

Mom's Parents, Frank
and Emma Ptacnik Valasek

Wedding Photo
January 27, 1902

Dad's parents, Peter
and Anna Michalski Zulkoski

Wedding photo,
February 19, 1900

MOM AND DAD STARTING THEIR LIFE TOGETHER.

They were proud of their car.

Wedding Photo
February 15, 1928

EARLY PICTURES OF ALYCE.

Alyce on the right holding her doll, pictured with cousins Marilee, Betty Ann, and baby Joseph

EARLY PICTURES OF GARY

A proud dad holding Gary.

Mom and baby Gary in front of the team of horses.

BEST FRIENDS!

In front of the
Tamarix Bush. It
had beautiful
feathery leaves,
tipped with pink
blossoms. A favorite
of Alyces'.

In the front yard amidst
flowers, weeds.

A rare studio picture of a
very small Alyce and Gary.

*Another pose in front of
the Tamarix Bush.*

*A reluctant pose taken at the
Burwell rodeo.
Note a hand on the right,
probably encouraging
us to sit still.*

*Dressed for church and probably
a visit to relatives one Sunday
morning.
Mom, Dad, Gary and Alyce.*

*Another pose,
another expression
in the studio picture.*

PROLOGUE

Forever Spring! Most of us think of spring as one of the seasons of the year. A long awaiting reawakening of our dormant environment. The outside world is taking on new life. The budding trees and flowers are awakening to the new season. The animal kingdom, the birds of the air are busily building nests. There is a feeling of new birth, a renewal of life's events, a new start, a fresh start.

As one grows older, one can become complacent, lethargic in anticipation of life's changes. It can become a habit to place much emphasis on the past, to recall those special memories that are somehow forever sealed in our very being, in our pores. We mustn't ignore or disregard them. Those memories are, after all, what brought us to where we are today. All the nurturing by our parents, relatives, teachers, and friends in our early days helped mold us for today. Whether those early days were warm, loving, cherished memories or whether they were unhappy, impoverished memories, it was that life that brought us to today. It helped mold our concepts, morals, faith, work ethic, all the avenues of our living, and thinking came out of that past life.

Why, then write a book about that past life? In recent years I've become more aware that the review of my early growing up days did have a huge impact on me, on the person I have become. I don't hold on tightly to those memories but I do hold on to them. I cherish those days growing up with a loving father, mother and brother. Also, I am hopeful that those who read this book will see value in preserving and sharing their own memories with family and friends. In so doing, perhaps there can be a lesson learned, working and playing together as family provides an enduring basis for achieving a truly satisfying life based on strong faith and moral values.

By recognizing where I came from, I also am able to discern where I am at this point in my life, where I want to be in the future. I have dreams yet unfulfilled. There are things to be done, books to read, countries to travel, families to see, games to play, books to write, recipes to try, hobbies to create, flower gardens to develop and rejoice in. Rather than think about moving from the fall of my life into winter, I find myself thinking about the 'spring of my life', looking forward with renewed joy, energy for a world yet to unfold. It is my choice. Forever Spring!

Table of Contents

Chapters	Title	Page
Chapter 1	Early Memories	1
Chapter 2	Neighbors	11
Chapter 3	Country Customs	15
Chapter 4	School Days	23
Chapter 5	Farm Chores	41
Chapter 6	Farm Animals and Pets	50
Chapter 7	Visiting With The Relatives	56
Chapter 8	Summer Time	65
Chapter 9	Summer School	72
Chapter 10	Getting Ready For Winter	76
Chapter 11	Entertainment	82
Chapter 12	Sunbonnets and Aprons	88
Chapter 13	Visiting Grandma Valasek in Kimball	90
Chapter 14	Remembering Christmas	95
Chapter 15	Remembering Easter	101
Chapter 16	Mom's Favorite Recipes	104
	Epilogue	121

Chapter 1

...early memories

What thanks can we give to God
for all the joy we feel in his presence because of you,
as we ask him fervently night and day
that we may see you face to face and remedy
any shortcomings in your faith?
~1 Thessalonians, 3:9-10

I heard dad call my name and felt his work worn hand gently shaking me awake. Before I opened my eyes, I could hear a strong wind howling and the heavy snow pelting the window and could sense that there was a major storm brewing. As I opened my eyes, the room was very light though it was still very early in the morning and the kerosene lamp had not been lit. The whiteness of the storm made everything bright. The outside world was indeed in the throes of a blizzard, not at all unusual for our part of the country. I think dad got a thrill in seeing my excitement when I found out that we kids could stay home, there would be no school. School was at least a mile and a half across fields, traveling to school would be impossible. I loved school but it was always exciting to stay home during bad weather. There was something awesome about a big blizzard, the loud whirling snow outside, and visibility at zero. Despite the treacherous weather outside, there was such a warm, cozy feeling inside. It was a time of staying near the heater, enjoying the closeness of family together. I doubt mom and dad were excited about a storm. It meant extra work, extra chores taking care of the farm animals, and probably a delay in some planned job that needed doing.

Mom and Dad were devoted to each other and the family. They lived a simple life saturated with hard times, enduring the great depression. There was always a sense of strong moral structure in our household. It wasn't talked about much but we kids grew up knowing right from wrong. We grew up in a faith filled environment We learned our prayers, we went to church on Sunday to St. Mary's Catholic church in Sargent, a seven mile drive. It's proper name is Assumption of the Blessed Virgin Mary. Church attendance was sporadic in my early days, mostly due to the lack of reliable transportation, poor roads and bad weather, but if the car would run and roads were passable, we did go to church.

I remember two, no, three incidents related with going to church when I was very young. One was remembering that there was a lot of water on the road, a flood actually. Roads were dirt or gravel and I remember Mom and Dad were very concerned. I don't recall how it turned out, how we got home, but I remember the water. The second incident, I remember coming home from church and my folks were talking about Pope Pius XI dying and we would have a new pope who happened to be Pope Pius XII. I guess I was about six years old and didn't really have any understanding about the significance of it but I knew from Mom and Dad's conversation that it was something important. The third incident I recall vividly even though I must have been very small. We were sitting in the back of the church on the left side and apparently I was being naughty because I remember my dad picking me up, carrying me outside and spanking me. I don't believe he had to take me out of church again after that. Strange how these little nuggets of memory linger.

The memory of waking up to the sounds of mom in the kitchen, the fragrant aroma of bacon, and eggs frying, bread being toasted, coffee perking are something that will stay with me always. I can still hear my parents talking together in the kitchen, sometimes in English, sometimes in Bohemian or Czech. I don't recall learning to speak and understand Czech. I just grew up in the environment and knew it. Sometimes as I got older I would listen in awe as mom and dad mingled the two languages. It never occurred to me that this was unusual, I just understood them.

It was always the custom to eat hearty breakfasts. The whole family was expected to get up and be at the table. Our family consisted of dad, mom, my brother Gerald, (Gary) and myself. Sometimes there would be ham or side pork. I always wanted soft fried eggs. I would dip the toast into the soft yellow yolk of the egg and thought it was absolutely delicious. I did not like the egg white however, and it was pretty much routine, mom would eat the white when I finished the yolk. Toast was made by placing a large slice of homemade bread onto a long kitchen fork and holding it over the open flame in the wood cook stove.

Sometimes she would make a special Czech dish called 'smorak.' It really didn't contain a lot of nutrients, flour, water, eggs and a pinch of salt, whipped together, then placed in a large greased skillet. As the mixture set, she would chop it up into small pieces with a small tin can that dad had sharpened one end. We would eat it with coffee. Even at a young age, when we had smorak, we kids got to have sweetened coffee with some cream added. We would eat the smorak by dipping a spoon of it into the coffee. We considered it a special treat. Probably not a dish a lot of people would like today, but one has to remember these were very poor times, people were creative in providing food for their families. This was a poplar dish in Bohemian families. I still have the sharpened tin can tucked away in my cupboard. When I see it, it brings back fond memories.

The storm gave Gary and me a chance to stay indoors and enjoy the warmth of our heater as we played all day. It was easy to play together or alone. Even at that young age, I had already learned to play many make believe games with my dolls. Most of the time Gary didn't want to play dolls, but he would play games with me. A favorite indoor game was 'hide the thimble.' Does anyone remember that simple game? One of us would hide the thimble and the other would look for it. It was great fun to call out 'cold' if he was far away from the thimble, or 'warm or hot' if he was near it. If we tired of that game, we might be creative and make a buzz saw by threading a long string through both eyes of a large button, tying the ends and holding on to each end of the string with the button in the middle, twirling it till it was tight then pull back and forth with each hand to make an elastic type motion that continued all the while we pulled on the string. Great fun unless it got close to our hair.

On these cold blustery days, mom would make what I thought were extra special meals. I don't suppose she thought they were, she just made what she thought would be good and hearty on a cold winter day. We could expect pancakes with lots of butter and warm syrup. We didn't have store bought syrup. Mom made a heavy syrup with sugar and water, added a maple flavoring, warmed it and we really enjoyed it. I still remember the piles of pancakes heaped on a platter. She made rather small pancakes, about the size of a cup but she made big stacks of them, usually three tall stacks on the serving plate. It's amazing how many we could eat. There would be fried eggs and crisp side pork. Mom would bake bread several times a week.

I still remember the baking pans she used. One was a 9" x 13" white enameled pan with a black trim around the edges that held three loaves. She also used two black tin single loaf pans. There were always five loaves of bread each baking day. I still have those pans, though mom is gone. Somehow, seeing the pans brings warm memories of her in those happy days.

For variety and again for the sake of economy, she would make 'baked milk bread.' She would fill the large white baking pan about one third with milk, add a bit of salt, then place small rounds of bread dough in neat rows to fill the pan, probably around fifteen. When it was baked, we would dish up a roll and some of the hot milk, usually turning the roll upside down with the milky side up. We would sprinkle it with cinnamon and sugar and thoroughly enjoy it. This would be our meal. There weren't any salads or other dishes. Mom might open a jar of canned peaches, apples or pears. Other times mom might surprise us with garlic toast. We didn't have electricity or a gas stove. We had a wood burning range in the kitchen. She would take one of the stove rings off the top to expose the flames, then with a long fork in a thick slice of homemade bread, she toasted both sides of the bread. She would immediately rub one side with garlic cloves, then butter it. What a treat. We would eat it with milk or on occasion we were allowed to have the sweetened, creamed coffee. Again, this was the entire meal. Sometimes there might be dessert but it wasn't a regular item in my early years.

Cornbread might be another meal. Sometimes mom would bake 'cracklings' into the top of it for added flavor. Cracklings were the fat that was rendered during hog butchering time. She would carefully cook down the fat pieces till they were crispy bits. She sprinkled it with salt. It was very rich and children weren't allowed to eat a lot of it alone but on the cornbread it was a special treat. We used to eat the large squares of cornbread with cold milk and sugar. I enjoyed the meal then and I still do.

Our small square house had a large kitchen that opened into a living room which was about the same size. The main bedroom opened off the kitchen. It was a very small room but held mom and dad's double bed and a smaller bed for Gary and me. It was tucked under the slanting bottom of the stairway that led to the attic. There was one window in the north wall. The west wall had a door leading to a small closet. This was a fascination for Gary and me as the closet had a door on the other wall that led into another small bedroom. What fun for two small children to create games crawling back and forth through the closet from room to room. That extra bedroom and the living room were not used in the winter time for a number of years or at least till we kids got older because it was a problem to heat the rooms. Winter times were spent almost entirely in the kitchen around the kitchen range or an upright heater in the north west corner. We didn't consider ourselves deprived as almost every other farm house conserved space and warmth in similar ways. It was the way of life at that time.

I don't really remember, but I suppose dad would get up early on those cold winter mornings and start the fire in the kitchen range so mom could cook breakfast. As I think about it now, it must have taken a lot of energy and commitment to do those tasks. I never heard them complain, they just knew it was the way to survive and care for each other and their family. Breakfast was always a hot meal. I don't think there ever was a consideration to doing otherwise.

Getting up and getting dressed was a chilly activity. As young children, we were allowed to come into the kitchen to get dressed by the stove or heater in the morning or to change into our pajamas at night. When we were older, occasionally, we might get to be in the living room. The large round heater was moved in to the north east corner and it was necessary to remain close around it to stay warm. Venturing out into the large living room was pretty chilly. We had a tendency to stand with our backs to the heater every once in awhile to take the chill off. In the evenings, mom or dad might make popcorn and it was comfortable in the warmth of the heater and with the family. Dad might read an old newspaper if we were lucky enough to have one, or maybe browse through the ever present Sears catalogue. Mom would sew, patch clothes by hand or at times she would do some embroidery or crocheting. That is

*Picture of the farmstead as it looked when Mom and Dad
moved on to the place, before any improvements were made
to the buildings or yard.
Immediate concern was simply to make a living
and survive the depression.*

*Early picture of Grandma Valasek's home in Custer County.
Note the sod house east of house.*

where I learned to do embroidery and crochet. I recall teaching myself. Mom was always busy so I studied directions and finally was able to teach myself.

Chapter 2

...neighbors

Love your fellow Christians always.
Do not neglect to show hospitality,
for by that means some have entertained angels
without knowing it.
~Hebrews 13:1-2

We lived in the country, with the nearest neighbors at least a mile or more away. There were quite a few neighbors in the area but at a distance. On a clear night, one could see the neighbors' lights in every direction from our place. In the winter, few people had cars that would start and if they did, the roads were probably not passable with deep snow. If someone did venture out with the car, they probably zigzagged across fields, avoiding snow drifts. Every so often, we would be surprised when a neighbor family would come to visit in the evening. They would come in a wagon drawn by a team of horses. We didn't have telephones so the visits were unannounced, always a surprise and always welcome. What fun to see them. If there were children, it was an especially fun time. Many times it might be older people. I got so that I really enjoyed being around the older people, listening to them talk.

One couple, Wayne and June Lewin visited fairly often. They would always bring June's elderly mother along. Her name was Eva Simpson. She was a favorite. I remember her thin wrinkled face, but mostly I remember her talking to me. She could tell the greatest tales about how her life used to be. I was intrigued. I could sit at her knees for hours listening. Wayne was a tall, thin man, rather shy but he loved to tease me. Mom curled my hair in those long curls that hung down. Wayne always said he would 'cut one off.' I remember really worrying about that and would run and hide under the bed when he came, at least when I was quite small. June was, and still is, a delightful lady, always cheerful, fun to listen to and talk with. I know mom considered her a good friend.

Sometimes the neighbors would walk the mile or more across the fields to come for a visit. We might hear our dog barking to announce that someone was approaching and soon we would see the light of a lantern as they made their way to our house. Before anyone went home, it was customary to serve a lunch. Despite the lack of modern conveniences, somehow mom always seemed to have a pie, or a cake handy. If she had been expecting company, she might serve sandwiches. Sandwiches were always made with ground meat, usually beef, sometimes pork or chicken, mixed with a relish, seasoned. They were quite good. I don't recall ever seeing slices of meat served in sandwiches during these early years. It seemed that hospitality and neighborliness always centered around lunches or meals. It seemed so comfortable to share food and friendship around the table. One has to recall that perhaps it is a custom that was first modeled around a table two thousand years ago as one man told his twelve to do as he did.

It would seem that perhaps many of the family problems that exist today might be resolved if they would once again get back to the custom of eating meals together, sharing the warmth and companionship of family.

On occasion, my folks would have Wayne and June for Sunday dinner or we were invited to their house. Something that strikes me strange today is that even though we didn't have a lot of modern conveniences at that time, mom and June always set a pretty table. I remember June putting out her best china, glassware, silverware and a pretty tablecloth. Mom would do the same. They made an effort to extend hospitality. They would always serve a large meal, all home cooked. Meat, potatoes, gravy, several vegetables, relishes, home churned butter and jams. Always there would be a dessert, most likely a lovely fruit pie. It seems a far-cry from the fast foods, plastic throw-a-ways many families now use.

Mom and June both loved their flower gardens. A tour of the yard was always expected and enjoyed as they looked at each other's flower beds. June's house and yard were surrounded with an array of beautiful flowers. Mom also enjoyed surrounding her yard with special flowers. I'm sure they exchanged ideas, seeds and probably plants. Such simple beauty was a source of joy and pride. They found beauty and contentment in their homes.

Chapter 3

...country customs

May God himself, who is our Father
and our Lord Jesus make our path
to you a straight one!
~1 Thessalonians, 3:11

It was customary for country folks to go to the town of Comstock every Saturday night. It was an important outing and a source of entertainment for the family. Men folk would wander down the street visiting with acquaintances as they walked around store to store. Conversations probably centered around their farm work, their crops, discussion about their few pieces of machinery. They were apt to stop in the creamery, the shoe repair shop, Wescott, Gibbon and Braggs, an all-purpose store, the barber shop, gas station. More than likely, dad would take some machinery in for repair at the Fricke Blacksmith shop at the west end of town.

A favorite gathering place for the men was Lebruska's Shoe Repair Shop. It was a small building on main street with a

THE MAP

Custer County, showing location of Comstock, Sargent, and the family farm midway between the two towns.

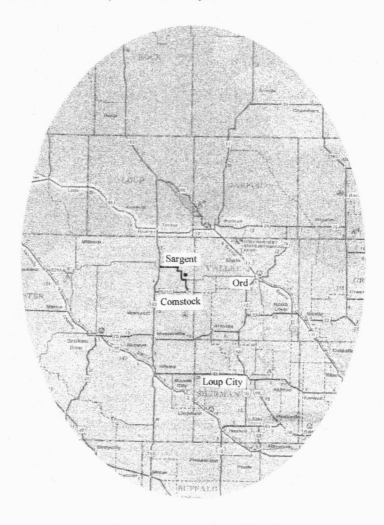

round heater with a number of chairs placed around the walls where men enjoyed sitting, visiting in the warmth of the heater on cold winter nights. The odor of leather was immediately evident as one entered the building. Almost everyone had shoes repaired, half-soling them, applying new heels, or stitching up tears. Few families could afford the luxury of new shoes when the old ones could still be repaired.

Shoes would be handed down from older child to a younger one. Unfortunately, many young feet were damaged by wearing ill-fitting shoes.

This was the place where I first saw a black man. He seemed very old to me, slight in build with a ring of fuzzy white hair around his shiny black head. His name was Billy Joe. Children were intrigued with him, liked to sit around him, and listen as he would tell them stories. Billy Joe was a respected gentleman, worked well for his employer.

Women would wander down the streets also, visiting as they went. To a small girl, it seemed like 'hours' when mom would stop to visit with an acquaintance, though I know now that it was probably only minutes.

Mom liked to browse in the Wescott, Gibbon and Braggs Store which was probably a forerunner to what we now know as our discount stores. There was a dry goods section in the east section of the store, groceries in the north section and to the west there was a pharmacy section. This area included an old fashioned ice cream parlor with the unique wire style tables and chairs. Women loved to browse in the dry good section, looking at dress material and the wide variety of thread and buttons.

The store used a cash register to exchange money but the billing was done on receipt pads with carbon paper inserts. Purchases were handwritten in pen or pencil on the pad, totaled, the store kept the original sheet, the customer received the carbon copy. It would be a while before adding machines would become commonplace.

Mom and dad had friends in Comstock by the name of Ochsner. John and Olga owned the main grocery store in town. It was customary to bring the week's collection of eggs to the store on Saturday night. At times they might take in two, thirty-dozen egg cases and one or two smaller twelve-dozen cases. Generally the eggs paid for all of mom's groceries each week. Dad would handle taking a can or two of cream to the creamery in town. He enjoyed being in the back of the grocery store visiting with John and other men folk that gathered there. Mom would go to some other stores to shop and visit with friends and neighbors but she would wander back to the grocery store and visit with Olga. They became friends as did Dad and John. The store was like many grocery stores of the time, filled with many of the staples farmers and city folks needed for their everyday meals. It was busy place, especially on Saturday nights, the main shopping day. I was always fascinated by the huge bunch of bananas hanging from a cord attached to the ceiling. As people selected some bananas, John or Olga would cut them off the huge stem with a curved shaped knife. If we were lucky, mom would get us a few bananas. It seems that in those days, fruit wasn't necessarily considered a staple, it was purchased only if money allowed for it.

Mom and dad and the Ochsners began visiting back and forth for Sunday dinners occasionally. I thought it was a great treat to be invited to the Ochsner's for dinner. They lived in town just across the alley south from their store. Visiting in a town home was always fun. Our family would go there after church, have dinner and generally stay for supper. It was a fun day, Olga always served wonderful food. She made a German dessert called 'kuchen' that we grew to love. It resembled a pie, with a crust, but the filling was sort of a custard with some fruit in it. Quite often it would be peach, but could be other berry fruit also. My mother got the recipe and it became an enjoyable dessert in our home too. Because we always had chores to do, milk cows, feed poultry and livestock, we always had to come home shortly after supper so that would end our visit.

My folks returned the favor and would invite the Ochsners to our farm home. This time it was mom's turn to cook a delicious meal. The meat would probably be fried chicken or roast pork or beef, always mashed potatoes and gravy, buttered corn or green beans, pickles, home baked bread and kolaches. But sometimes she would fix pork chops or chicken fried steaks. She would coat them with seasoned flour, fry till a crispy golden brown and tender. We all loved the steaks or chops. As usual, we would also enjoy supper and maybe play cards afterwards. Our family experienced a great sadness when the Ochsner's young son, John Dean died rather suddenly. Later on they had a daughter and another son. I always looked forward to playing with LeAnn and Danny.

Gary and I had one favorite place we liked to visit in Comstock. It was the Lukesh Creamery and Ice Cream Parlor. Folks would leave their cans of cream there while they went to shop at the grocery store and other stores in town. When it was time to go home, we would stop at the creamery to pick up our cans and money from the sale. Mary Lukesh, the owner of the creamery was a cousin of my mothers and she always treated us kids kindly. She might have a lunch for us before we went home. As they visited, she would wash down her creamery equipment. One of the things she did was scrape down the large ice cream cartons that were nearly empty. As Mary emptied the last fragments of ice cream, she would give it to Gary and me. I still have fond memories of enjoying the ice cream in that little building. Years later when I drove through Comstock and saw the building, I was startled to see how tiny it really was. I have to wonder how she could do the creamery and ice cream business in that tiny building, and maintain a small kitchen in the rear. The one thing that stands out in my memory is the joy we all experienced in our visits to this friendly business establishment.

Evelyn Visek, a friend about the same age as me, enjoyed going to grade school together. It became a habit for the two of us to plan on meeting each other in Comstock on Saturday night. We loved to walk the streets, talk about our school, spin dreams of who we wanted to be when we grew up, discuss the movie stars, generally just wandering around town enjoying each others company. It was fun to meet up with other friends and neighbors doing the same thing.

As we got older, occasionally we were lucky enough to get a dime from our fathers and go to the ice cream parlor section of Wescott, Gibbons and Braggs store and order a chocolate sundae. I remember one Saturday night especially well. After we finished our sundae, Evelyn and I were still hungry for more ice cream so we dared find our fathers and ask for another dime. Much to our delight and surprise, we got the dimes and enjoyed a second chocolate sundae. Those probably were the best sundaes I ever ate. I regret that I lost contact with Evelyn after we graduated from high school.

Just as in those early years, the country people went to Comstock on Saturday nights, it was also the custom to go to Sargent on Thursday afternoons. Sargent was about seven miles north west of our farm. Thursday was traditionally sale day. Livestock, cattle and hogs were sent to market. Men enjoyed sitting in the sale barn watching the sale and visiting with one another. Sargent was a bit larger community than Comstock, and had more stores. The women and children enjoyed walking the streets in good weather, visiting. You'll notice I mention visiting a great deal. In this era there were few newspapers, no television, occasionally there were radios in some homes, few had telephones so people depended on visiting with each other to catch up on the news in other families as well as any news people had from around the county, state or country. Going to town was considered entertainment. It was a long time before we were to experience the saturation of news media we now have in our homes.

Chapter 4

...school days

For nothing is impossible with God.
~Luke 1:37

Grade school was a wonderful experience for me most of the time except my very first day visiting there. I remember the first time I was in Longwood school, a small country school house located two miles from home. If we cut across the fields, which we usually did, it was about one and a half miles. Children almost always walked to school, it was a rare treat if we would get a ride.

Longwood School, Dist #6

My first recollection about the school was with my mother when she took me with her to pick up Gary after school. I think she may have been enrolling me for first grade the next year. At any rate, it was 'art time' and the teacher had handed out the lesson to the children. The teacher gave the older children a picture of a basket as well as several kinds of fruit to color. Then they were to

Longwood School, Dist #6

make a fruit basket by pasting the fruit into it. Being a small child, she gave me a picture of a basket already filled with fruit to color. As I started to color I noticed the other children with their individual fruits. It seemed exciting to see them cut and paste. I remember thinking that I should cut up my basket of fruit also, then paste it together like the big kids. The teacher came by and mildly reprimanded me, she said I was not supposed to cut it up, she had given me an easy task for a child my age. I remember being embarrassed. Maybe for the first time. I didn't know I had done something wrong and was surprised to be told about it. Strange that memory has stayed with me many years later. (Today, March 18, 2000, I just read in the paper that this teacher, Rosie Brim Chalupa died this week. A sadness touches my heart.)

Getting ready for school in the fall was a great adventure. We rarely got to buy novelty things like coloring books, pencils and crayons during the year but when school was to begin, we got to go to the store and pick out one red Big Chief writing tablet, a small box of new crayons (I think there were eight colors in the box) and a new pencil. Sometimes we also got a new eraser. One year we got to buy a pencil box that held those special treasures. I remember vividly one year we got a double-deck pencil box. The top layer had the usual little compartments for pencils, eraser, etc. There was a pull-out drawer in the bottom layer, sort of a secret drawer. I think that is where I kept my crayons. Such a simple memory but it must have made an impression on me, receiving such a cherished item and rarely was I thrilled with a gift as much as I was with that little pencil box.

School was so exciting to me. It was fun to dress for school. It was even fun to walk the mile and a half to school. Gary and I cut across fields, across fences, and neighbor's fields. Dad had walked the route with us, making certain we knew what landmarks we should use as guides and offering some cautions. The cautions became especially important a few years later when an irrigation ditch was dug through the fields. Gary and I thought it was fun to walk along the bank of the ditch all the way to the school but I know our parents were forever worried that we might be tempted to play in it. It was far to deep for youngsters our age to play in.

As we walked to school, Gary and I would have great times talking about things we wanted, spin dreams. I especially remember one year when we both dreamed of having a pony for Christmas. Actually, I think the dream was for a nice, big riding horse. We even dreamed of getting a great new saddle,

Alyce in front of the school

Gary and Alyce ready to walk the mile and a half to school.
Note the dog, always a constant companion on the farm.

bridle, etc.   We could hardly wait for Christmas. It was Christmas eve. Uncle Mike came over for a visit earlier in the evening which was a bit unusual, especially on Christmas eve. It wasn't till a long time later we discovered the reason for his visit. I don't recall what gifts we got under the tree but I do remember there was a note on the tree saying something about looking outside, the gift was too big to bring in. We went to the door and there tied to the door knob was a small brown and white spotted Shetland pony. It was winter, it was cold, there was snow on the ground but Gary dressed only in his pajamas jumped on the pony and rode around the yard.   It never occurred us at the time that Uncle Mike had made a special effort to walk across the fields to bring the little pony for us. What a thrill that Christmas was. Somehow all those dreams of a grand, big riding horse with a bright new saddle and bridle were forgotten.   We were so thrilled with 'Tiny', the little Shetland pony. There is a lesson there for all of us. *We tend to give our children exactly what they want, sometimes go to great lengths to find just the right toy to fulfill there every dream, yet perhaps wise parents might make better choices if they would let their children experience dreams with surprising results.*

I'm sure it was very hard for my folks to provide us kids with clothes for school. Most parents had the same problem during these very poor times. There wasn't any thought of 'style', everyone seemed just happy to have decent clothes to wear. I remember going into a second-hand shop in Ord with mom to look for some items. I still remember a cute little bright red cardigan sweater that buttoned all the way down the front. It didn't matter to me that it was not new, it was new to me and I could hardly wait to wear it to school. I wanted to wear it all the time. I also remember mom and I stopping in to visit the Chalupsky's in the west end of Comstock. They gave me a pair of little tan boots with a fur cuff along the top. They laced up front and I thought they were the most wonderful shoes I had ever had. I do think my folks had problems getting me to stop wearing them when they got too small.

My love for books began in the first grade and continues to this day. It was such a thrill when I realized I could read. I still remember my first primer, Dick and Jane. "Dick, see  Dick, see Dick run". "Jane, see Jane, see Jane run". After reading a few pages, Dick said "Come, Father. Come and See." Jane said, "Come, Mother. Come and see." Baby said, "See, see!" At this point the teacher asked me, "what do you think they see?" I said "airplane". As I turned the page, I was so thrilled to see that it was an airplane. In those days, the airplane was still awesome to most of us. There were very few airplanes flying over our part of the country. If we heard one, everyone in the house usually would dash out of the house to watch it.

Years later when the little country school was sold as well as all its furnishings, I bought the complete set of Elson-Gray's Basic Readers which includes the Dick and Jane primer. It is one of my most cherished possessions.

There was a small library located above a small niche above the downstairs steps at Longwood. It was so exciting to look through the books, and on occasion we got to check one out to take home. At one time there was a traveling library that the school subscribed to. I read many books through this service.

A nice surprise when I was about ten years old and in the fifth grade. One evening, mom and dad mentioned that they thought I should begin using the correct spelling of my name. It had always been Alice Ann up till then. They said the spelling on my birth certificate was 'Alyce Ann.' I could hardly wait to get to school the next day to tell my teacher and classmates about my new name. It wasn't until I went to college when the 'Ann' was dropped but to this day, if someone calls me 'Alyce Ann,' I know it is a relative or someone from my early years.

I looked forward to lunch time. For a long time, our lunch pails were little, round tin honey buckets. Usually there was a sandwich or a hard cooked egg or a tomato and some fruit. It was fun to sit with other children eating lunch. In a few years my folks bought us real lunch pails. Mine was a yellow-gold color, Gary's was pale green. They were oval in shape with a nice lid that came off. Wire bands located on either side of the pails were folded up over the pail as handles and held the lid in place. Gary and I still have those little pails. Now they hold so many memories.

In later years, mom began going to some homemaker or extension meetings put on by the county extension service. She learned all kinds of lunch box 'tricks'. She learned to make pepper and salt straws by rolling a bit of waxed paper, then creasing the ends to close them. She liked to send the seasonings with us especially if we had tomatoes or hard cooked eggs for lunch. After we got an icebox, she learned to freeze some desserts and then they were 'just right' for eating at noon. She also learned to make some new sandwich fillings that she also chilled overnight. I think it would be rare for us to bring any leftovers home. At one point, the school received 'commodities' to serve the children at lunch. I remember there were tall cans of grapefruit juice, pork and beans, crackers and Mrs. Grass' noodle soup. I think everyone was excited when the students mothers and teacher first started making the soup. A dehydrated soup was a novelty and probably the greatest novelty was the little butter egg. It was great fun to add the water, watch it come to a boil and see the 'egg' melt. It was good soup.

Most of the children looked forward to recess and lunch times at school. One of our favorite games was playing softball. This was interesting because the children were all ages, all sizes. There might be only one or two children in any one grade so we played together as best we could, with varying ages and talents. I was the only one in my class all of my first eight years of grade school. Sometimes we played hide and seek. There were usually tall weeds along the edges of the school ground and a row of trees so we found some great hiding places. One time my friend, Evelyn and I lay down in the tall weeds, and weren't found until the school bell rang when lunch time was over. We thought that was a great stunt. I think our teacher was getting a little worried about where we were as she couldn't find us either. We also played a lot of hopscotch though I think that mostly we played it at home especially when some of the cousins might be there.

Periodically, there were evening activities at school, it might be a program by the children for a special holiday, it might be a PTA meeting or some sort of party or get-together. Always there was a social afterwards. There would always be pies and cakes, probably some ground meat sandwiches and beverages.

Ladies took special care to bring very nice items, almost a

personal challenge to bring a very nice cake or delicious pie. An all-time favorite was the Box Lunch Social. Ladies and girls would fix a special boxed lunch, decorate it prettily. Everyone would gaze at the assortment of lovely boxed lunches. One of the men would auction off each box hoping to make some money for the school budget. Women hoped their husbands would buy their box. Girls would hope a certain boy would buy theirs. It was a fun time. Not infrequently whether by mistake or on purpose, men and boys bought boxes other then their wives or girl friends.

I think I liked everything about school, reading, arithmetic, geography, history, art, penmanship and music. I think it was Friday afternoons when we had a sing-a-long. It was such fun to sing 'Little Brown Church in the Vale', 'The Old Oaken Bucket', 'Oh Where, Oh Where Has My Little Dog Gone?', 'Billy Boy', 'The Farmer's In The Dell'. 'Little Brown Jug', 'Wait For the Wagon', 'The Quilting Party', 'Over The River And Through The Woods'. I don't hear these songs anymore. I wonder, do they sing those in school these days? I think the first song I remember ever hearing was 'My Bonnie Lies Over the Ocean'. Another song that remains in my memory is 'A Tisket, A Tasket, A Red and Yellow Basket'. My twin cousins, Irene and Ilene Visek were singing it at a program in school. I can still hear those young girls as they sang that song, maybe some of the fascination was to see two girls who looked alike. I don't remember if those were the titles of the songs, but the lyrics remain with me.

I also remember two poems by Robert Louis Stevenson. Both of them held a special fascination for me and I still remember many of the words. Part of the fascination probably was the illustrations with the poems. My little girl mind could fashion wonderful dreams as I read the poems.

The Swing

How do you like to up in a swing,
Up in the air so blue?
Oh, I do think it the pleasantest thing
Ever a child can do!

Up in the air and over the wall,
Till I can see so wide,
Rivers and trees and cattle and all
Over the countryside.

Till I look down on the garden green,
Down on the roof so brown,
Up in the air I go flying again,
Up in the air and down!

My Shadow

I have a little shadow that goes in and out with me,
And what can be the use of him is more then I can see;
He is very, very like me from the heels up to the head;
And I see him jump before me, when I jump into my bed.

The funniest thing about him is the way he likes to grow,
Not at all like proper children, which is always very slow;
For he sometimes shoots up taller like an India-rubber ball,
And sometimes gets so little that there's none of him at all.

He hasn't got a notion of how children ought to play,
And can only make a fool of me in every sort of way.
He stays so close beside me, he's a coward you can see;
I'd think shame to stick to nursie
as that shadow sticks to me!

One morning, very early, before the sun was up,
I rose and found the shining dew on every buttercup;
But my lazy little shadow, like an arrant sleepyhead,
Had stayed at home beside me and was fast asleep in bed.

There were special days of the week that we would have a penmanship class and an art class. In penmanship class, we would try to copy special samples of cursive writing, many examples of letter formations. I think I enjoyed the class though somehow through the years, I proved that I would never be a beautiful hand writer. I tend to scrawl large badly shaped letters.

Art class was a fun time for most students. We especially looked forward to the holiday seasons. Art always included the current holiday. Do any of you remember what great fun it was to color the pictures of Easter bunnies and eggs, Santa Claus, the colorful Thanksgiving turkey and the Halloween pumpkins? Even Arbor Day, New Years, President Lincoln and President Washington became subjects of art work. As a child, we rarely saw colorful pictures of the various holidays the way we do now, until the holiday was drawing near. Being able to color pictures in vivid colors was so exciting. My young mind could visualize the colorful Easter bunny hiding my goodies, or Santa coming silently into my house to leave me a prized gift as I labored over a colorful picture. What fun to color the orange pumpkins or the colorful turkeys. I remember being in awe as I colored pictures of Presidents Lincoln and Washington. At the time they were more imaginary then real people.

Longwood School, District #6
Comstock, Nebraska

1937-38   **Teacher:** Miss Rosie Brim
            County Superintendent: Harry E. Weekly

George Haynes	8th Grade
Anton Hvezda	8th Grade
Marcella Shanks	8th Grade
Irene Visek	8th Grade
Elmer Jo Kluna	7th Grade
Gene McKimmey	7th Grade
Stanley Vitek	7th Grade

Wayne McKimmey	5th Grade
Emily Kriss	4th Grade
Eldon McKimmey	4th Grade
Norma Skolil	3rd Grade
Ellen McKimmey	2nd Grade
Donita McKimmey	1st Grade
Lourene Boro	4th Grade
Ilene Visek	7th Grade
Maggie Warner	7th Grade
Clara Belle Warner	7th Grade
Leonard Warner	5th Grade
Gladys Warner	4th Grade
Dolly Warner	1st Grade
Gerald Zulkoski	1st Grade

1938-1939 Teacher: Miss Rosie Brim
County Superintendent: Harry E. Weekly

Elmer Kluna	8th Grade
Gene McKimmey	8th Grade
Ilene Visek	8th Grade
Stanley Visek	8th Grade
Clara Belle Warner	8th Grade
Maggie Warner	8th Grade
Wayne McKimmey	6th Grade
Lourene Boro	5th Grade
Emily Kriss	5th Grade
Eldon McKimmey	5th Grade
Leonard Warner	5th Grade
Gladys Warner	4th Grade
Ellen McKimmey	3rd Grade

Donita McKimmey	2nd Grade
Dolly Warner	2nd Grade
Gerald Zulkoski	2nd Grade
Billy McKimmey	1st Grade
Alice Zulkoski	1st Grade

1939-1940 Teacher: Miss Rosie Brim
County Superintendent: Gerald A. Thurman

Clara Belle Warner	8th Grade
Wayne McKimmey	7th Grade
Hubert Arlinghous	7th Grade
Lourene Boro	6th Grade
Emily Kriss	6th Grade
Eldon McKimmey	6th Grade
Leonard Warner	6th Grade
Rose Marie Arlinghouse	6th Grade
Herman Arlinghous	5th Grade
Gladys Warner	5th Grade
Ellen McKimmey	4th Grade
Donita McKimmey	3rd Grade
Dolly Warner	3rd Grade
Gerald Zulkoski	3rd Grade
Billy McKimmey	2nd Grade
Alice Zulkoski	2nd Grade
Alfreda Arlinghous	1st Grade
Evelyn Visek	1st Grade
Fritz Warner	1st Grade

1940-1941 Teacher: Mr. George Hlavinka,
County Superintendent: Gerald A. Thurman

Hubert Arlinghous	8th Grade
Rosie Marie Arlinghous	7th Grade
Lourene Boro	7th Grade
Emily Kriss	7th Grade
Herman Arlinghous	6th Grade
Gerald Zulkoski	4th Grade
Alice Zulkoski	3rd Grade
Evelyn Visek	3rd Grade
Alfreda Arlinghous	2nd Grade
Margaret Boro	1st Grade
Hilda Visek	Kindergarten
Norman Kriss	Kindergarten
Shirley Skolil	Kindergarten

1941-1942 Teacher: Miss Martha Olson
Mrs. Vera Plock
Miss Margaret Pester

County Superintendent: Gerald A. Thurmam

Wanda Kriss	Kindergarten
Rosalie Visek	Kindergarten
Larry Waldman	Kindergarten
Margaret Boro	1st Grade
Norman Kriss	1st Grade
Shirley Skolil	1st Grade
Hilda Visek	1st Grade
Evelyn Visek	3rd Grade
Alice Ann Kulkoski	4th Grade
Gerald Zulkoski	5th Grade
Norma Skolil	7th Grade
Lourene Boro	8th Grade

Emily Kriss	8th Grade
Edward Silver	8th Grade

1942-1943   **Teacher:** Mrs. Freda Kokes
County Superintendent: Gerald Thurman

Norma Skolil	8th Grade
Gerald Kulkowski	6th Grade
Alice Ann Zulkowski	5th Grade
Evelyn Visek	4th Grade
Margaret Boro	2nd Grade
Hilda Visek	2nd Grade
Shirley Skolil	2nd Grade
Norman Kriss	2nd Grade
Rosalie Visek	1st Grade
Larry Waldman	1st Grade
Wanda Kriss	1st Grade

1943-1944   **Teacher:** Mrs. Ruth Lenstrom
County Superintendent: Gerald A. Thurman

Gerald Zulkoski	7th Grade
Alice Ann Zulkoski	6th Grade
Ruby Snell	6th Grade
Evenyn Visek	5th Grade
Richard Travis	4th Grade
Hilda Visek	3rd Grade
Margaret Boro	3rd Grade
Shirley Skolil	3rd Grade
Norman Kriss	3rd Grade
Rosalie Visek	2nd Grade
Larry Waldman	2nd Grade
Wanda Kriss 2nd Grade	

1944-1945   **Teacher:** Mrs. Arline Shanks
County Superintendent: Gerald A. Thurman

Gerald Zulkoski	8th Grade
Alice Ann Zulkoski	7th Grade
Evelyn Visek	6th Grade
Ruby Snell	(moved)
Hilda Visek	4th Grade
Norman Kriss	4th Grade
Rosalie Visek	3rd Grade
Larry Waldman	3rd Grade
Wanda Kriss	2nd Grade
Roger Snell	(moved)

1945-1946   **Teacher:** Mrs. Arline Shanks
County Superintendent: Mary Gilmore

Alice A. Zulkoski	8th Grade
Evelyn Visek	7th Grade
Irene Snyder	6th Grade
Hilda Visek	5th Grade
Norman Kriss	5th Grade
Gilford Snyder	5th Grade
Rosalie Visek	4th Grade
Roscella Snyder	4th Grade
Larry Waldman	4th Grade
Dwayne Anderson	3rd Grade
Wanda Kriss	1st Grade

Chapter 5

...farm chores

Whatever you do, work at it with your whole being.
Do it for the Lord rather than for men,
since you will know full well you will receive
an inheritance from him in your reward.
~Colossians, 3: 23-24

When we got home from school, Gary and I usually had to help with chores. It meant feeding the pigs, helping 'bucket' feed the baby calves. This was great fun but sometimes a little hazardous. Dad would pour some milk in small buckets and us kids would hold them while calves would drink from them. Sometimes the calves were very frisky and would 'root their heads' into the pails and nearly send us flying. Mostly it was fun to be around the young calves. They had been weaned from their mothers so we could milk the cows and have cream to sell.

We usually had ducks and geese. Mom would set eggs under some contented hens, waiting for the ducklings and goslings to hatch.   What an exciting time when the eggs would began to crack and the little beaks would peck out of the shells.   There is nothing prettier then soft, fuzzy newborn ducklings and goslings, also nothing as noisily distracting.   I still recall seeing the cracked shell scattered around the nests and the characteristic odor accompanying the hatching. A chore Gary and I had was to wander in the fields to bring a certain weed called 'nettles' to the little ducklings and goslings.   The plants were a bit prickly to handle but we really didn't mind picking them because we knew that the ducklings and goslings would gobble them down with gusto.   It was fun to hold the bunches while they would gobble   it up in minutes.

Every spring mom would order baby chicks. I'm not certain how many but surely over a hundred. She favored the White Plymouth Rock chicken because they were a meatier chicken and also seemed to lay more eggs. She never liked the White Leghorn chicken as it was a thinner, rangy type. What a thrill when those chicks arrived. They came in boxes, about 2'x2' and 6" deep. There were dividers in the boxes making 4 smaller spaces. Holes the size of quarters allowed the chicks to breath. First she would carefully clean and sterilize the brooder house, make sure she had enough watering jars, feeders and a heater. This was a round tin canopy suspended from the ceiling, hanging about 12 to 18 inches above the floor over a small kerosene heater. It was important to provide adequate heat for baby chicks because if it was too cool, they tended to bunch close together to get warm and a frequent occurrence could be the suffocation of some chicks. Mom would not want to lose even one chick. The heater was always a concern and risk. Mom and dad always worried about a fire.

I loved to help mom feed the chicks. Once a day she would spread newspapers on the floor in the brooder house and sprinkle cracked corn (we called it 'scratch'). How the chicks loved it. I can still hear the scratching noise as the many chicks scrambled onto the newspapers, peeping away as they ate. The rest of the time there were a number of long narrow feeders placed around the brooder house filled with a mixture of soft grains called "mash". Quart jars were filled with water, turned upside down over little glass trays that allowed the water to seep down slowly as the chicks drank the water. It was our kids job to keep the jars filled. As a youngster, it was sometimes tricky to flip the full jar upside down on with the little glass tray intact and not spill the water. Well, once in a while we did.

Mom did try to raise turkeys for a few years but they were usually more trouble than other poultry. They tended to fly out of their pens, land atop buildings. They always seemed to need extra attention, such as special medications for certain ailments they seemed to get. Mom or dad would hold the turkeys' head snugly while they pushed a large pill down their throat. It seems there wasn't any other way to give them that particular medicine and it was quite a chore to do. Turkeys aren't the friendliest creatures, they can get pretty aggressive with their legs and wings.

Occasionally a hen would make a nest somewhere in one of the buildings, lay her eggs and hatch out her own batch of chicks. Every so often, we would be surprised when a hen would come wandering into the yard leading a batch of baby chicks. This was always a surprise and fun to watch the mother hen as she wandered abut the yard, protecting her chicks, scrounging for food. If you've never seen a mother hen protect her chicks, it is quite a unique experience. If she senses danger, she clucks and the chicks scurry under her. She fluffs out her feathers so that they are completely hidden, not a chick is visible.

There always seemed to be hogs on the farm. Dad would always have a few sows and raise litters of pigs. He seemed to take a special interest in caring for them, rarely did we kids help with the hog chores. One reason of course, a sow could be very vicious, very protective of her new litter of pigs. It was fun to go see the little piglets, just like most newborn animals, they were very cute. Dad always enjoyed wandering through the stalls, checking on them, making sure all could nurse properly. Occasionally, a runt (a tiny piglet) wasn't able to compete with the others so dad would bring it into the house so we could help it get started drinking milk, keep it warm, and safe. Gary and I probably thought we had a good pet, but it wouldn't last long. As soon as it learned to eat, and get around well, it had to go back out with its' mother.

Alyce and Gary taking turns to sit on Dad's riding horse, Jerry.
Note the barefeet, common during the summer months.

Dad with his sows and young pigs in the lot east of the barn.
Dad loved to stand in the feed lots, gazing at his cattle and hogs.

Stacking alfalfa hay was a chore that dad usually shared with his brother Mike, and a neighborhood friend, Wayne Lewin who lived on neighboring farms. Dad would rake the alfalfa into windrows. A couple of the men would load the hayrack, using pitchforks to toss the hay up as high as they could reach. Then they had to unload it on the stacker forklift. The stacker was in position with a team of horses ready to pull the forklift up and toss the load of alfalfa onto the growing pile. The trick was to have the team of horses move at a steady pace, then stop at exactly the right spot so the hay would land in the middle of the pile. Too fast a pace, or jerking at the end of the pace would toss the load too far to one side of the stack or occasionally clear off the pile. That made extra work for the man on top of the stack trying to level off the top before the next load came in. As I got big enough, I got to drive the stacker team and eventually became quite good at it. That didn't mean that occasionally I didn't make a mistake and toss the load too far. Wayne liked to tease me. Stacking was hard, manual labor for everyone.

Dad had very little machinery and what he did have was old, seemed to need constant repair. There were times when he would need a bolt or a nut to fix something but did not have a nickel to buy it. The same could be said of the family car. At best it seemed to always be a problem to start it. Dad would stand in front of the car and crank and crank until finally some loud sputtering as it would start up. Keeping tires repaired was another chore. I remember standing by while dad would remove the intertube from the tire, dip it in water until he would find the leak, use the special compound to seal and patch the tube. If I was with dad when he was doing repairs on machinery or the car, I could expect to be asked to run an errand, go find a certain wrench or whatever he needed. It made me feel important to be helping.

When the irrigation canal was dug across our farm, it created a whole new way of farming. It also created a great deal more work. Dad learned how to use the survey telescope to find level ground to dig small irrigation canals across the end of his fields. The first irrigation pipes were actually wooden. He bought three inch wide laths and nailed four of them together to make long boxes or wooden troughs used to run water from the irrigation ditch into rows of corn. We would dig a space in the side of the ditch, lay the wooden trough in it and hurriedly cover it up. Water would then run to the end of the row of corn, usually it took one day and night. Generally the troughs were set every two or three rows of corn, then each day we would have to dig a small channel from the watered row to a dry row next to it. We called it 'changing the water'. As soon as Gary and I were old enough, we had to help with changing the water. Mom frequently helped also. I don't know how many wooden troughs dad made that first year, but it seemed like a lot. It was labor intensive work. Of course when the irrigating season was over we would have to pick up all of the wood troughs and store them till next year. Some years later, aluminum pipes became available and were much easier to handle and maintain.

Wash day was an all day job. Mom would get up early, put water on the cook stove to heat. I think she and dad filled containers or tubs the night before and set them on the range so the water would be heating and handy the next morning. I remember seeing mom use the wash board to wash clothes. Later, she had a wash machine with a gas motor. This was a great improvement but frequently needed some tinkering by dad to keep it running.   When the clothes were through washing, she would run them through the wringer which we ran by turning a crank. Mom often had us kids help with that chore but we had to be careful, if we got our fingers in the wet clothes too close to the wringer, we sometimes 'howled' as our fingers got caught and went into the wringer. Clothes from the wringer went into a couple of tubs of rinse water and through the wringer again, then finally they were ready to hang on the clothes line south of the house. One of the rinse tubs always had bluing in it, so that clothes would be sparkling white. Mom had great pride in doing each job the best way she could. I think there were four long clothes lines and generally mom had them hung full of clothes on wash day.

On hot summer days, they dried quite rapidly and could be brought in the house. Starched clothes had to sprinkled and rolled up and tucked away in a bundle wrapped in a heavy cover for ironing the next day. Clothes, towels, bed linen, etc. that didn't need to be sprinkled were folded carefully. Mom liked to starch her pillow cases, dresses, shirts, aprons, tablecloths and dresser scarves. I wonder how many women iron their pillow cases today. Even with the nice materials, most would look nicer with a little pressing.

There used to be a saying among country women. Monday is washday, Tuesday is ironing day, Wednesday is mending day, Thursday is market day, Friday is cleaning day, Saturday is baking day and Sunday you go to church. Most neighbors seemed to abide by the routine. One could see a number of the neighbors' homes from our farm yard, and you could expect to see clothes on their lines every Monday morning. Women took pride in having their wash hanging on the line early in the morning. I do think the women had sort of a race to have theirs out first and more than likely, mom's was one of the first.

Chapter 6

...farm animals and pets

Look at the birds in the sky.
They do not sow or reap,
they gather nothing into barns;
Yet your heavenly Father feeds them.
Are you not more important then they?
~Matthew 6:26

We always had pets, almost always a large dog that helped with the cattle. It was customary to always have several cats because farm buildings always had mice. Sometimes we would have a dog or cat that became a special pet. One time at Longwood school, a large gold colored cat came onto the playground. All of the kids at school were excited about the pretty cat. I remember that Gary and I ended up taking it home with us, how we happened to get it instead of one of the other children, I don't remember. I know we hoped we would get to keep it, and we did. We almost always named our farm animals but for some reason I don't remember what we called this gold cat. I know she was very large and really fun to have.

We had a little terrier dog named "Boots". He was quite small, tan in color. I enjoyed having him around but he was sort of a scrappy dog, tended to bark a lot. I was small and much of the time I was afraid of him. I remember that I would climb up on the chairs to get away from him. I'm not certain that he would have bitten me but he did scare me. We didn't have him for long, he suddenly became ill and died. Later we got another rat terrier. Casey was also small, white with black spots and turned out to be the family favorite. He seemed to be exceptionally smart, very friendly. At one point we said he could 'almost talk'. Casey seemed to understand whatever we were saying or ask him to do. If we were out doing chores or working in the fields with our folks, Casey was there too. He always seemed excited to be around our family members. He loved to go with me to get our mail, about a quarter of a mile from the house. If I said, "You want to go get the mail?" he would be down the road ahead of me. Unfortunately, one day as he excitedly got to the mailbox before me, dancing around in the road, a car hit him, he died instantly. I know our entire family grieved for that cute little dog.

Sometimes one or more of the cats would have a nest in the barn. Dad would tell us that they would have kittens so we would watch anxiously. Finally the day would come when we could look into their nest and see the tiny kittens. There is nothing like a newborn kitten. They are so tiny, so helpless, their eyes are still shut and they have a characteristic tiny 'mew' sound. They sound like a distressed baby. Once their eyes are open, they start wandering about, just cute fuzzy little balls.

We always milked around eight to ten cows, sometimes more or less. I remember begging to help milk the cows but would be told that I was too small. Then finally one day, dad said I could give it a try. At first it was fun, though quite a challenge to learn the technique, but it wasn't long before the novelty wore off and I realized this was going to be work. After the milking was done, the milk was run through a separator in the milk house. The separator had a large storage tank, rotating disks in a smaller bowl that were turned rapidly with a crank. The revolving force separated the cream through a drain into a container and the milk through a drain into another container. The process was a bit more complicated then that but it is the general idea of how milk and cream were separated. Cream was stored in large cream cans in the cool cellar until Saturday night when we took it to the creamery to be sold. Milk was used for the household and the excess fed to the 'bucket calves' or little pigs or mixed with mash for the sows and other hogs.

Of course, cleaning the separator was a big chore morning and evening. After all the milk had been run through the separator, water would be run through to give it an initial rinse. But then it had to be taken apart, all the many discs and drains so they could be properly washed with soap and water and ready for the next use. One would not dare leave it sit as the residue milk would sour in the many parts.

When Gary and I were small, one of our parents, usually mom would go with us into the pasture to get the cows. We would usually go later in the afternoon so we would get home at a certain time in the early evening to milk the cows. We always named all of our milk cows. There would be Polly, Jersey, Daisy, Dolly, Guernsey, Pansy and so on. When we went after the cattle, we always knew which ones were missing. The pasture was large, quite hilly, we often had to hunt for the cattle. Sometimes they had a favorite place, such as a shady, grassy draw. Other times, they might be clear in the back of the pasture. I think it was probably a mile. Because the cattle and we generally walked along certain trails, there were some well defined paths or deep ruts from the constant use. It was especially fun to go in late summer when there would be wild fruit on various shrubs. There was a canyon along the east side of the pasture that was especially good for finding fruit. Sometimes there would be wild raspberries, gooseberries, elderberries.

One time along the hill side, there was a large patch of currant shrubs that was covered with small, red currants. Currant shrubs have grayish leaves on medium tall, hard wood branches. We really enjoyed them but I remember it was the only year that it had the berries. Closer to the barn, there were some wild plum bushes growing in a draw. We frequently went there to pick a few to eat. If there were a lot of them, mom would come with us to pick a large quantity so she could make plum butter. We didn't have store bought jellies and jams so this was a real treat for us. On rare occasions, we would find a patch of wild strawberries. As dad was able to have larger herds of cattle in the pasture, the fruit shrubs were gradually destroyed by the grazing cattle.

I always enjoyed looking at the flowers in the pasture. It was always a surprise where one might see some, in a draw, along the paths, or tucked in crevices along the hill sides. There were wild roses, usually in a delicate pink. There would be a profusion of pasture primrose, bluebells, asters, sunflowers, goldenrod's, flax, alfalfa, clovers, and numerous other wild flowers. There was also a variety of cactus flowers. The yucca cactus with its tall clusters of bell flowers dotted the hill sides, as well as some prickly pear cactus. Cactus always had beautiful flowers.

My favorite shrubs around the house were the wild yellow rose and the old fashioned lilac bushes. Each had the distinct aroma, so sweet and symbolic of spring. When I happen to be around one of those bushes now, it immediately takes me back to my early days on the farm as a little girl sniffing the rose or lilac bushes. I expect that is where I gained my love for flowers. I was always picking bouquets for the table. I still do that. People who know me well, know that if there are flowers outside, I am sure to bring some inside.

Sometimes mom would give us a snack before we went to the pasture. I remember one time we were standing behind the barn getting ready to go get the cows in the pasture. She brought Gary and I some fresh baked bread and some lovely red jam. It looked so good but one bite and I immediately took a dislike for it. It was tomato jam. I refused to eat it. Many years later an elderly friend, Margaret Rea said she had made some tomato jam and wanted me to have some. I thought "it's been many years since I had that first taste, I guess I could try it again." My first bite of the bread and jam and took me right back behind the barn where I had that first taste. I still disliked it. It probably is the only food I dislike and probably always will.

Chapter 7

...visiting with the relatives

Men do not light a lamp and then put it under a bushel basket.
They set it on a stand so that it gives light to all in the house.
In the same way, your light must shine before men so that they
may see goodness in your acts and give praise
to your heavenly Father.
~Matthew 5:15-16

Occasionally we would drive to Loup City to visit Aunt Emma (mom's sister), Uncle Bill and their son Donnie. We kids thought it was great fun to visit our aunt in the town. It seemed like Aunt Emma and Uncle Bill had such a wonderful house, kitchen cabinets, indoor plumbing, a gas stove, refrigerator and electric lights and even a sidewalk and lawn. She always seemed to have lunch for us. Quite often it would be bologna or cold cuts and cheese. I had never tasted store bought cheese before and it seemed like I couldn't get enough of it. One time she had a soft cheese spread that she had made melting cheese and cream together. It was the first version of what we now know as cheese whiz. Mom started making it too. What a great treat that was. At that time hard cheese came in big five pound wooden boxes. It was always a thrill when mom and dad could afford to buy a box. Years later when I was in Loup City and drove by aunt Emma's house I was amazed at how small it was.

Uncle Bill owned the hardware store in Loup City and was known as a successful business man. He also began the propane gas service. At one point my folks had arranged to get a propane refrigerator from him, had it installed and when Gary and I got home from school that day, mom and dad were fairly bursting to show us the 'surprise'. It surely made kitchen life a lot easier for mom and fun for all of us too. We began making some frozen desserts, salads and best of all, there were ice cubes. Before the refrigerator, we did have an icebox for a while. We would have to buy blocks of ice, make sure the drain pan was emptied often or it ran over. It certainly served its purpose at the time. I remember before we had the icebox, Jell-O became available in the stores. Mom would mix it up and set it under a pan in the shade on the north side of the house. It generally took all

I remember Uncle Bill always wore a suit, a tie and hat. Uncle Bill, Aunt Emma, Cousin Donnie.

day to set but, my it was good. Sometimes if we were lucky we might have a banana to slice into it.

AT GRANDPA PETE'S FARM

Mom, Dad, Gary, and Alyce in front of the house.

Grandpa Pete with a favorite horse and pipe.

In front of the barn, Grandpa Pete and Uncle Sal (Sylvester) ready to go to the fields with the horses and mules hitched to the wagons.

We also visited dads' family on a farm south west of Loup City. Grandpa Pete, Uncle Paul and Aunt Julie lived there. I always liked going there, it was about a three to four mile drive across pasture trails to get to their house from Loup City. It was a fairly large two story home and surprisingly, there were a number of rather nice out-buildings, a good sized barn. Dad's side of the family seemed to get together fairly often. Aunts, uncles and numerous cousins from around the Ord and Elyria communities would gather for dinner and supper on weekends, usually Sunday. Everyone chipped in, bringing food. Those were good times. I still remember Aunt Julie going out to butcher more chickens in the afternoon so there would be enough for the evening meal. Making meals was labor intensive, generally being made the day of the dinner. Prepared meals,

Pictured at frequent gatherings of family for Sunday visits. Shown in the front row, Gary, Alyce, Aunt Julie, Aunt Anne and Mom. Back row, Grandpa Pete, Uncle Mike, Aunt Marthann, Uncle Paul, Uncle Charles and Dad.

Years later, a picture of Grandpa Pete with his family, Mike, Anne, Julia, Cookie (Lucille), Casper, and Paul.

frozen meals or refrigerated foods weren't heard of. Women expected to prepare the food as it was needed. They baked their own breads, rolls, pies, cakes, cookies, etc.

My Aunt Mary (mom's sister), Uncle Joe Visek and their children Betty Ann, Marilee and Joseph lived on a farm west of Comstock. It was about five miles, southwest across the country road from the Douglas Grove Cemetery. I don't know how often our families got together, but it seemed like we were together quite often, despite difficulty traveling. Second hand cars didn't start or run well, roads were poor, money scarce for gas or tires but somehow, the families managed to connect fairly often for visits. I have so many good memories playing with my cousins at their place or at our home. Betty Ann and Marilee were a bit older than Gary and me, and Joseph was the youngest but we just had fun being together. One time when we were all quite young their house burned down and for a while until Aunt Mary and Uncle Joe could rebuild a house, they lived in a small round building. I remember we were there around Christmas time, it was very crowded but no one seemed to mind. There was always good food and visiting. At some point I remember the men

Uncle Joe and Aunt Mary Visek with their children, Betty Ann, Marilee and Joseph.

said they thought they heard a noise on the roof, maybe it was Santa. Sure enough, us kids heard it too with much excitement. Interestingly I don't recall anything further. I do remember my brother, Gary wearing a navy cap, it was knitted, fit like a helmet over his forehead, with earflaps. I remember thinking it was such a wonderful cap. Girls in those days wore parkas, usually knit in bright colors that fit down over the ears, tied under the chin. Getting a new one for Christmas was always exciting. I remember I could hardly wait to go to school and show everyone what a wonderful present I got and of course my school mates did the same thing. We cherished anything new.

It seemed that Aunt Mary and her family and Aunt Emma and her family would visit in our home fairly often, probably on Sundays. They would spend the whole day. The adults would visit, the women making the meals while they visited. In those

A Sunday visit to our farm, from the left, Aunt Mary and Uncle Joe Visek, Mom and Dad, Aunt Emma and Uncle Bill Vodehnal.

days, it would be rare for the men to come into the kitchen to help. They would spend their time together, walking around the farm or just relaxing in the yard or in the living room. After a meal, the women worked together again cleaning up, doing the dishes. The men would go back to visiting. We kids found many things to do around the farm. It was great fun to climb up into the hayloft of the barn. The ladder up into the loft was a challenge in itself, certainly scary for us smaller children but we wouldn't want to let it show. We wanted to keep up with the big kids. You never knew what would be found up there, sometimes nests of baby chicks, or new kittens. Always, we would see lots of sparrows and pigeons. The boys liked to shoot the sparrows but we didn't like to see them do that. We had to be careful in the hayloft, there were open spaces above the cow stalls that were used to toss hay down to the cows. One could easily make a mistake or misstep and fall down.

A favorite game was hopscotch. We kids could spend hours tossing the little pebble into the various spaces and hop around. I regret that Gary and I and the other cousins didn't get well acquainted with two cousins that lived in western Nebraska, in the Kimball area. Uncle John and Aunt Nellie live on farms in the area and had two sons, Leonard and John. Because it was a great distance to travel and because the boys were considerably younger then the rest of us, we didn't get together very often. When we were able to make the trip to Kimball, it was always exciting to see our younger cousins.

COUSINS

*Marilee Visek, Gary and Alyce
with Aunt Julia.*

*Mom holding Joseph.
From left, Betty Ann and
Marilee Visek, Alyce and Gary.*

*Betty Ann, Marilee, Gary, Donnie, Alyce and
Joseph with enough pets or dolls to go around.*

John and Leonard Valasek
in front of their farm home
in Kimball.

Mom with Alyce, Gary
and Donnie. BB Guns
were a cherished
toy by the boys.

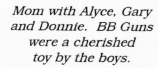

Alyce, Donnie, Betty
Ann, Marilee, Gary
and Joseph. What
memories this group
of cousins have of the
many get-togethers
we shared.

Chapter 8

...summer time

Which of you by worrying can add a moment
to your life-span? As for clothes, why be concerned?
Learn a lesson from the way wild flowers grow.
They do not work; they do not spin..
Yet I assure you, not even Solomon
in all his splendor was arrayed like one of these.
~Matthew 6:27-29

When school was out in the summer, it seemed that summer vacation went on forever. We played so much but also helped with work. As we were older, Gary and I helped shock grain. Strange, we always seemed to beg to be able to do certain chores then soon found out it was hard work. Shocking grain was not only hard work, it was hot, dirty work. Bundles of grain were dropped in rows across the fields. There was usually someone in the neighborhood who owned a binder and would hire out to most farmers in the area. Dad would hire his grain done in this way. The binder would mow and bind the grain into a fair sized bundles, dropping them along the field as it moved along.

It would take my mom and dad, Gary and me several days and evenings to shock all the fields. We were taught to take two bundles, stand them up against each other, then take two more bundles and stand them on opposite sides making sort of a tent with the four bundles. Usually we would add four or more bundles in upright positions around the first four. The idea was to stand the bundles up so the grain would be off the ground and stay dry. We always took a big crockery water jug with us placing it in a shock to keep it cool. Sometimes we had problems remembering where we left it. Shocking grain was a hot, dirty job. I remember being dusty, scratched from the chafe, having mosquito bites. It was part of the job. All of us were thrilled when a whole field was 'shocked' and all those little grain tents stood waiting to be hauled in for threshing.

Most neighbors were doing the same thing. We could see them in their fields shocking the grain. There seemed to be a sense of excitement at harvest time, a time when farmers finally would reap the reward of their hard work all summer. Then it was threshing time. We didn't have combines, few could own that expensive machinery. A thresher would come through the neighborhood going from farm to farm. Neighbors helped neighbors. Some of the men and boys brought hayracks and picked up the bundles of grain from the shocks, others helped unload bundles into the threshing machine, some helped stack the hay that resulted, and others unloaded the grain into bins as the wagons were filled. I can still see my dad unloading the grain into the storage bin, methodically scoop by scoop. How hard it must have been and how hot he was, but there also was a satisfaction that only another farmer would understand.

Several women would usually get together to help fix the big noon meal because there could be as many as 12 to 14 men expecting to eat. There were always piles of fried chicken, mashed potatoes, creamy chicken gravy, stacks of fresh sliced tomatoes, probably green beans or corn, sliced cucumbers and always some kind of pickles and always home baked bread. It was a big day for the ladies, too. The chickens had to be killed and dressed early in the morning. All the cooking was done on a hot range. There were no fans. Windows were open to help move air. Sometimes the men choose to squat on their feet in the yard in the shade of the trees rather then sit in the house to eat.

Despite the heat and hard work, it didn't stop the men from a bit of horse play to break the monotony. It seemed there was one fellow they always liked to pick on. You could count on Junior being chased until they caught and dumped him in the stock tank. He probably didn't mind too much. Dad would bring a block of ice from the ice house, make some chips so we could make cool tea for the men. One time my cousin was pouring tea for the men and she just happened to pick a certain fellow and just happened to pour a goodly amount down his back collar. That created a bit of excitement.

Threshing went on till dark so the ladies had to fix supper for the men also. It would be more fried chicken, probably potato salad, more tomatoes. I know dad was always happy when his grain was safely harvested and in the grain bins. Mom was happy that the rush to fix big meals was over. But their work wasn't finished because dad would follow the thresher to the next farm to help out his neighbor until all the neighbors' grain was harvested. Mom returned the favor to a couple of the ladies who helped her out. Despite the hard work, probably most of the men and women enjoyed a certain camaraderie, visiting with each other as they worked.

Mom always had a huge vegetable garden and somehow always managed to have a fair variety of flowers around the house. I remember especially the gladiolas she grew. I thought they were the most beautiful flowers on their tall stalks. Also, she grew dahlias a few times. I think we all were in awe of those huge beautiful blossoms. Of course there were potatoes, tomatoes, green beans, peas, sweet corn, onion, beets, green peppers, cabbage, kohlrabi, cucumbers, herbs, strawberries. She loved to look through the seed catalogues, pick out the routine vegetables she always planted, but sometimes she surprised us with an unusual selection. I remember one time she tried to grow peanuts, though not too successfully. I know we kids were disappointed because we were certain there would be big clusters of peanuts, just like the pictures in the catalogue.

There was a period of a few years when mom had a large strawberry patch east of the house. We had a bumper crop of berries, huge dishpans full. We had all the fresh berries we wanted to eat with sweet cream and sugar and she also made large batches of jam. That was a wonderful time, despite the need for frequent picking. Also, dad always insisted on having winter squash, both the Hubbard and acorn variety as well as cantaloupes and watermelon. We kids got our share of hoeing the weeds and watering the gardens.

We depended on the garden for fresh food all summer but then mom always canned large quantities to carry us through the winter. I remember sitting in front of the house in the shade helping mom string and tip green beans or strip the pea pods. There would usually be bushel baskets of the vegetables so it was a long process. Dad used to plant the melons in among the sweet corn. That way he could use the same ground for both crops. We never wasted very much, mom would save the watermelon rinds and make sweet pickles out of them. She and the neighbor ladies prided themselves on making this wonderful relish. Dad liked the big Hubbard squash but I always preferred the small acorn squash.

One chore Gary and I had was to pick potato bugs. They don't hurt one, but certainly did do damage to the plants so dad would fix a little can of kerosene for each of us and we would walk down the rows of potatoes, picking as many as we could see. Dad would give us a penny a bug. We thought it was a great way to make some spending money.

In the fall before school would began, there were times when the wind blew huge piles of thistles into the fields. The only way to get rid of them was to burn them. In the evening, dad and mom would take us kids along into the fields while they lit the thistles. I expect it was a bit scary for my folks to see such big fires blazing but I know Gary and I thought it was great fun. We even got to help take pitch forks and move stray thistles into the blaze. They would make a great sizzling, cracking sound and then they were gone. Only blackened soil remained ready for dad to prepare the soil for another harvest in the spring.

Harvesting corn was an exhausting, difficult job. All of it had to be shucked by hand. Dad would hitch up a couple of reliable horses to a wagon outfitted with tall side boards on one side. He and mom would go out early in the morning and shuck corn till they filled the wagon. It usually was very cold, maybe some snow on the ground. They wore special heavy sleeves pulled up past their elbows to save wear on their coats. Each of them wore corn shuckers or huskers on one hand. It was a small leather strap with a sharp hook they used to strip the corn husks from the ears before they tossed it into the wagon. I'm not certain of the actual name of it but remember it was important for them to use it. As they tossed corn into the wagon, the ears would hit the tall side boards, fall into the wagon. I don't remember if us kids were kept home on purpose or because it was too cold to go to school, but we would be bundled up in the front of the wagon while they picked the corn. Sometimes dad would playfully toss an ear of corn on us. Usually it would take most of the morning to fill a wagon, then dad would unload it while mom would go into the house to fix dinner. She would probably open a jar of canned beef, make a gravy out of it, serve it on mashed potatoes or thick slick of bread. Canned beef gravy is a memorable food, enjoyed by everyone.

It was quite a hectic, busy, tiring routine, but mom and dad worked together, each doing their jobs. It is hard to imagine that they worked so hard, struggling to make a living, yet seemingly to enjoy life.

Chapter 9

...summer school

On the way of wisdom I direct you, I lead you on
straightforward paths. When you walk,
your step will not be impeded,
and should you run, you will not stumble.
Hold fast to instruction, never let her go;
Keep her for she is your life.
~Proverbs 4:11-13

Summer school was really religion classes at the church in Sargent. While us kids were in grade school we went every summer for two weeks. The priest would have two Franciscan nuns come teach the classes. I still remember the first ones, Sister Fabian and Sister Borgia. Sister Fabian taught the little children so she was my teacher and the first nun that I knew. I remember being so in 'awe of her'. She wore a full length habit which was the long brown dress, a long black or brown apron, the white around her face and a black veil that hung in back. The little children had their class in the sacristy, a little room behind the altar that was used by the priest to store all the vestments, liturgical supplies and where he dressed for Mass. It

Young Priest, Father Michael Szczesny

seemed so inspiring and divine to be there. Occasionally Father Michael Szczesny (Father Mike) would stop in to speak to us, usually ask some questions and again I felt such awe.

The first priest I ever knew was Father Mike. He was a tall, dark, handsome man with a very proper, traditional carriage. I never saw him in anything but his black suit and collar. Through the years I had few occasions to see him, however, in 1997, at the Chrism Mass in North Platte, he was honored for sixty years in the priesthood. I was able to take my mother to the Mass and when Father Mike saw her, he immediately hurried over to visit with her. They had a wonderful conversation, renewing their friendship. She

Years later, a reunion of Mom and Father Mike at his 60th Ordination Anniversary Celebration in North Platte

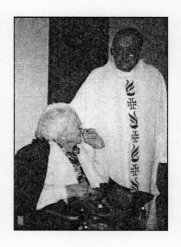

was 92, he in his 80's. Two dear old friends enjoying their reunion. He now lives in Crown Point, Indiana.

Another priest that made an impression on my young life was Father Thomas Siudowski, (Father Tom). He and Father Mike both came from the Chicago area and were good friends. Father Tom was later appointed Monsignor, and happened to be the pastor of St. Patrick's Church in North Platte when I moved there in 1960. He died August 7, 1991. I was privileged to attend his funeral in the cathedral in Grand Island. Both priests made a lasting impression on my life, surely influential in my faith life.

Sometimes Sister would take us into the church, let us walk around the sanctuary and the altar. This was pre-Vatican II and a time in our church when parishioners, other then those involved in liturgical celebrations (lectors, servers, etc.) were generally not privileged to go into the sanctuary area. In those days there seemed such a mystery, such a hushed awesome feeling in those church spaces. I remember having such a special feeling of wonder maybe a bit spell-bound by being in the very presence of this sacred place. Occasionally if we did our lessons well, Sister would give us a prayer card of one of the saints. Also, we might be given a medal of a saint. These were very special gifts to us, we always took special care of them. I still have many of them. One summer, Mom and Dad arranged for us to stay in town with the Garwick family who were sending their children to summer school. Gary and I were a little older then and it saved folks from having to drive us to and from the classes each day. Mrs. Garwick had rented a house in town and allowed us to stay with them during the two week period. After class each day, she would let us play, and often we walked around town, sometimes visiting some of her acquaintances. Being in town was very special to me. Being a little girl, the town seemed very big, exciting.

There was another year that my folks arranged for us to ride to summer school with Vencil Visek. He and his folks, Jim and Sophie Visek lived on a neighboring farm less then two miles from us. Sophie was my mom's aunt. Vencil worked in Sargent at the lumber yard every day so us kids got to ride with him. I think his twin sisters, Ilene and Irene also went to summer school. I remember one particular evening before we went home, Vencil stopped at the little ice cream parlor, bought a pint of strawberry ice cream. He gave each of us the little wooden paddle spoons (used at that time) and we all dug into the pint. Needless to say, none of us got a lot, but it surely was a wonderful treat.   Another one of those little nuggets that lingers in my memory.

Chapter 10

...getting ready for winter

A harvest of justice is sown in peace for those
who will cultivate peace.
~James 3:18

In the fall, there was a special day when mom and dad would begin hustling to bring in vegetables that were still in the garden. They seemed to have a special insight that it was the night there would be a hard freeze. We didn't have frequent, current updates of weather as is the custom now. If the radio did work, the weather reports were less then current and hardly helpful. As soon as we got home from school, we kids would hurry and help Mom and Dad. Usually that would be the squash and melons, probably the last of the tomatoes and onions. We might also dig up the last of the carrots and parsnip. We would work late in the night to be sure we had every thing in. Potatoes probably had already been dug and were safely in the cellar. It would be cold work, but we all worked rapidly to bring everything into the safety of the warm cellar.

There was a great satisfaction to have the harvest done, knowing we would have wonderful meals during the cold winter days. I remember coming into the warm house after all that work, mom would have baked squash, probably side pork and home baked bread for supper. Mom always filled the centers of the squash with butter, brown sugar or honey. I continue to make my squash that way to this day. It tasted so good and we all seemed to sense a deep satisfaction in knowing a good harvest was stored for the winter. It was so satisfying to see the baskets of potatoes, carrots, squash, onions lined up in the cellar and to see the shelves fairly bending with the hundreds of jars of canned vegetables and fruit mom had preserved.

Everyday household items used in the kitchen.

Getting ready to butcher a pork was a busy, exciting time. Usually dad would have a neighbor or relative help him with the actual slaughter and scalding of the pig. We kids weren't allowed to be around until it was time to dress out the pork. Almost every part was salvaged for something. Mom would want the head for making a special Bohemian sausage called 'iternici' (jaternice). She would also make 'jelitha' (jelita) which was a blood sausage, enjoyed by most older Bohemian people. Pig's feet and knuckles were kept to make a pickled delicacy called sultz. Much of the pork cuts would be stored in a salted crock. Side pork was thickly cut. Oh, how good that was. Mom would be busy all day sorting through the many cuts of pork. She would even save the scraps of fat cut off of the meat and render it slowly till it was crisp and crackling. It would be used to flavor some baked foods. The lard was saved for baking. We didn't worry about cholesterol in those days. Dad would be helping. We always knew on butchering day that we would have a great supper that evening. The fresh pork was so good.

Making the iternici and jelitha was a huge project always done in the winter so they could be stored in the cold. I've included the recipes in the back of this book. It was always interesting to watch mom make the mixture, she would taste it frequently to be sure she had just the right flavor. After mom would have the mixtures the way she wanted, she would prepare the casings. She carefully scrapped and cleaned them. Dad had a sausage stuffing piece of equipment, consisted of a container about two gallon in size. A spout extended from the bottom on one side. A lid that fit the opening had a heavy screwed handle fitted to its center. When the container was filled with the sausage mixture, the lid fit over the top. A casing was fitted to the spout and with care, the lid was screwed downward, forcing the stuffing into the casing. It took a lot of coordination and care to be certain the casing didn't slip off the spout. When one long casing was full, mom or dad would take string and tie it tightly at measured spaces to make separate sausages. There always had to be two ties close together so each sausage could be cut apart separately. Mom would then put them in boiling stock for about twenty minutes, then hang them on rods to cool and dry. The best way to eat them was to place them in a hot oven, bake until the casing was crispy. This was one of the great Bohemian treats. We all loved them. I've eaten itenici made by a number of people, including Grandma Valasek, but I always thought my mom's were the best. They had a characteristic flavor the others lacked. I believe garlic was the secret ingredient.

Butchering beef was another big project. Dad would always make sure the beef had been well fed so that we would have good meat. Preserving beef was a totally different process than pork. Meat was cut up into small pieces, placed on roasting pans and browned in the oven. Then mom would can the meat with a beef broth. Probably nothing compares with beef and gravy made from canned beef. Many meals were comprised of heaping mounds of mashed potatoes, the canned beef and gravy and whatever garden vegetable was available. It might be corn, green beans, carrots or peas. Invariably, they would be creamed with rich country cream. There might also be turnips, beets, kohlrabi, squash or cabbage. Later on when the grocery store in Comstock installed a deep freeze unit, mom and dad would take their beef and pork to the store to be processed and frozen.

That was the end of the beef canning. I'm certain mom was relieved of the huge task of canning, but we did miss the marvelous flavor of the home canned beef.

Churning butter was a weekly chore that Gary or I had the privilege of doing. As kids, we thought it was a very long, tiring time before we began to see the flecks of butter forming. A bit longer and it soon became a huge chunk of butter. Mom would take over, remove the butter to a large pan, wash it in cold water, sprinkle it with salt and using a wide wooden butter paddle, she would work it until all the moisture was squeezed out. It was then placed in a brown crock and stored in a cool place. We could drink the buttermilk or it was saved for buttermilk pancakes or biscuits.

Coffee was a main beverage for adults but seemed to be served mostly at mealtimes or the rare social events. There didn't seem to be 'coffee breaks' like we know them now. My first memories of coffee was that we had to grind the beans. We had a little square wooden grinder, the beans would be put in the top, a handle was turned to grind the beans into a little drawer in the bottom. The only fun part of grinding the beans was being able to open the drawer and see how much coffee I had ground. I remember it as being another very tedious chore, it seemed to take a long time to grind a drawer full.

Mom sewed most of our clothes. She really was a very good seamstress. She made many dresses and blouses for me, shirts for dad and Gary, pajamas and always dresses and aprons for herself. She rarely had a store bought dress. The neighbor ladies and relatives loved to trade patterns, also, they enjoyed a 'new style' one of them might have. It was an economical measure also as patterns would cost a nickel or sometimes as much as a dime. In later years, mom made clothes for her grandchildren, did a lot of mending for the grandsons.

One other job mom did was make homemade soap. She would put together a mixture of fat, lye and water, cooking it to a certain consistency, pour it into flat pans to cool and gel, then cut into bars. To use for washing clothes, she would either shave thin slivers so it would dissolve easily or she would tie some bars into a thin bag and put into the washing machine. She claimed it washed clothes the cleanest and brightest. I think she must have been right because our clothes were always very clean.

Saturday night baths were a ritual. A small round bath tub was placed in the living room near the heater. Dad would carry in cold water, then as water heated on the stove, it was added to make a warm bath for us. We kids got to bathe first, sometimes there was a bit of a 'skirmish' of who would bathe first or who 'did not want to bathe at all'. Mom arranged towels or sheets on the backs of chairs around the tub so we would have extra warmth and a bit of privacy.

Chapter 11

...entertainment

Do not neglect the gift you received when,
as a result of prophecy, the presbyters laid
their hands on you.
~1 Timothy 4:14

Who could forget the Hugo shows? The Hugo Players were a tour summer tent show. It is said that the show first went on the road in 1908 and continued touring central Nebraska each year until 1953. They began coming to Sargent every year. They would come to town with numerous bright, decorated trailers to haul their props. A huge tent would go up at the east end of town, their trailers would be parked all around. Bright colored posters were up all over town. A certain excitement would build in town as time drew near for the shows to begin. The Hugo Players usually stayed in town for a whole week.

Some people made an effort to go every night. I don't recall how often we got to go but I think possibly a couple of times during the week. At the time, admission was ten cents, quite a bit when dad had to buy four tickets for us. It was exciting to see the different acts, the different actors, the special music. Everyone enjoyed listening to the honky tonk music and the popular hits of the day played on the brightly painted 'Tin-Pan Alley' piano. The actors usually presented a skit every night, the popular tragedies, murder mysteries, comedies and occasionally a sentimental romantic play. Audiences enjoyed cheering the hero or heroine, would boo or hiss the villain, applaud the rescuer of the down trodden. Almost as popular as the show were the candy sales during intermission. Usually the boxed salt-water taffy contained a novelty prize or coupons for redeemable gifts. Cast members went through the audience hawking the candy and prizes. It was a time when candies and little surprise gifts were a novelty for people in our part of the country. It was great fun to watch the excitement and on a rare occasion, dad might buy a box for us kids. Each year we looked forward to certain actors. We all remembered Harry the dad, his wife Stella and young Herbie. It was fascinating to watch the actors and actresses in their beautiful costumes, clothes I had never seen before. There always were some comedy acts, hilarious skits and occasionally a little magic. And then the show would be over, the entire cast would come on stage to sing the sentimental 'Goodnight, Goodbye' or 'Ring Down the Curtain, We've Got the Blues on the Run'. Maybe we would get to see them next year.

Nebraska's Big Rodeo at Burwell was an annual event. At the time, it was the biggest western, cowboy entertainment in the state. Huge crowds came every year. Burwell was a distance from our home, about twenty five miles, quite a way to drive on gravel roads with poor cars. Mom and dad tried to have the farm work and chores caught up so we could make the trip to the rodeo. We knew it would be a day-long trip. Mom and I would get picnic food ready, always fried chicken, potato salad, sliced tomatoes, bread and some sort of drink, maybe a cool lemonade. What excitement for us kids as we drove closer to Burwell. We could see the Ferris wheel and other rides in the distance.

The fair grounds were on the east edge of town and as we drove along, we saw Indian teepees. What a strange sight for us little kids to see all these marvelously colored people in bright Indian dress. There were many little children running around among pretty ponies. When we parked at a distance and walked into the fairgrounds, mom and dad took us kids past the Indian campsite. Hanging on branches, we saw long strips of beef jerky drying. We thought viewing the Indian camp was the highlight of the trip.   Gary and I had read about people of different cultures in our Exploring American Neighbors Geography book, but we never realized we would get to see any of them.

As mom and dad walked us through the fairway, through the carnival area, a whole new world of excitement and color opened up to Gary and me. All kinds of bright lights, loud music, games, fortune tellers, rides, foods, drinks. One time Gary and I had our picture taken. We still have it. Often, mom and dad would meet an acquaintance and stop to visit. One time as I waited for mom to finish her visit, I noticed a gypsy dressed in her bright colors and jewelry beckoning for Gary to come to her. I became frightened and ran to mom. Of course nothing happened but I remember being frightened by someone of another culture.

It was time for our noon lunch, all that wonderful food mom and I packed. We sat in the shade of our car, enjoying our lunch as many other people were doing the same thing. The big event was about to began, the big rodeo. We found our seats in the grandstand, watched all the special riders, the trick riders, the clowns, the big parade of cowboys, an Indian dance and finally the rodeo with all its events. Excitement for small children, of course. Gary and I talked about it for days.

Occasionally, mom and dad would go dancing at the Bohemian National Hall out in the country west of Ord. They would take us kids along. It was great fun, there was always a large crowd. Good Bohemian music, waltzes and polkas. Little kids would race around on the slick dance floor, skating or dancing. When we got tired, sometimes mom and dad would fix a place for us to sleep on folding chairs behind the orchestra. Once in a while I would feel some naughty kid pinch me while I tried to sleep. Other times, mom and dad would let us sleep in our car. They would come out occasionally to see that we were okay. I know they enjoyed a chance to visit with friends and to dance. There's nothing like a good Bohemian dance to make one feel good.

We created our own entertainment. Sometimes when dad was away from home till late at night, mom would come outdoors with us kids and we would all lie on the ground looking up into the dark sky. We would shout out 'I spy' when we saw the first star and then whenever a new star appeared. Finally, the sky would be full of stars and we would have to quit, but that was so enjoyable, being with mom and the connection with nature.

Such simple joys. On hot summer days, sometimes mom would cut an orange in half and give the halves to Gary and me. What a treat to have fruit in the middle of the week. Occasionally, when we were in the cellar north of the house, mom would mix some Ovaltine, milk and a bit of sugar in a tin shaker, shake it up, then give us kids a cup to drink. Because Ovaltine was expensive, it was a rare treat. Another enjoyable snack was a large slice of home baked bread, spread with very thick cream, sprinkled heavily with sugar. It was something that was usually available and we did enjoy it. Mom was very creative with providing an occasional snack, it generally was a pleasant surprise and something that didn't happen daily or often. The few snacks that might be available in the stores were usually too expensive. Dad might on a rare occasion come home from town with a small bag of chocolate star candies, or chocolate covered peanuts, candy corn or my favorite, the gummy orange slices.

The reason dad would go to town during the week was in need of a machinery repair or to have the blacksmith shop make a repair. Besides bringing candy, he might surprise us with a large package of wieners or bologna. I know mom was especially pleased to have the tasty, ready to cook meats. Served with thick slices of homemade bread, the whole family always enjoyed these meals.

Chapter 12

...sunbonnets and aprons

But as for you, be strong and do not relax,
for your work shall be rewarded.
~2 Chronicles 15:7

I hadn't thought about sunbonnets and aprons for this book, but one day as I happened to be watching a re-run of "The Little House on the Prairie" show, I noticed Ma Ingalls, Laura and Mary Ingalls wearing sunbonnets and I immediately remembered how important they were to mom when we kids were little. She always wore a pretty print bonnet whenever she went outdoors. She made small ones for me and expected me to wear one too. All farm women and girls wore them.

Without realizing it, the women were way ahead of their time providing good skin protection, perhaps eliminating skin problems and cancer in later life. Their objective at the time, however; was not a health concern, it was primarily to keep their skin clear and white or light. It was considered unattractive for women and girls to have dark, tanned skin. Women would sew bonnets to match their print dresses. Usually they would have an everyday one, to do yard work or chores. They would reserve a newer, attractive one for special occasions like visiting neighbors or, yes, they wore them to town. Most women did.

All women wore aprons while they cooked or did chores. Obviously, it was to help keep their dresses clean longer. They would not think of cooking or cleaning without wearing one. Also it was easier to wash and iron an apron then an entire dress. They wore full aprons, or ones that covered most of the front of dresses. As times became a bit easier and there was a bit more money, the women enjoyed having an assortment of aprons. They loved to trade patterns. I think most women kept a clean, starched apron hanging behind the kitchen door or a nearby closet so if unexpected company showed up, they would hurriedly whisk out the clean apron. Though these were poor, difficult times, women took a great deal of pride in their appearance.

Chapter 13

...visiting Grandma Valasek
in Kimball!

A cheerful glance brings joy to the heart;
Good news invigorates the bones.
~Proverbs 15:30

My earliest memory of Grandma Valasek was that she lived far away in Kimball, a small town in western Nebraska. My uncles Frank and Joe lived with her. Another uncle John and his wife, aunt Nellie also lived in the area on a farm. As I recall, my folks tried to visit them once a year. It didn't always happen because money was scarce and the Model A car didn't always run very well. It took a lot of planning to arrange to drive the long distance to spend a few days. Mom would carefully pack a big lunch to take along since this would be a day-long trip. All of us were excited as we drove along, through the small towns, and especially to observe the trains that generally ran close to the road. Frequently, we would spend time counting the cars on the many trains that went by.

All of us enjoyed the Burma Shave signs along the roadside. I don't know how often they appeared but we always watched for them, read them and enjoyed a chuckle. I remember one sign: The bearded devil-was forced to dwell-in the only place-where they don't sell-Burma Shave! Another sign: If you drive-while you're drunk-carry your coffin-in your trunk-Burma Shave! Another sign: In this world-of toil and sin-your head goes bald-but not your chin-Burma Shave. And so they went, such fun to drive along, hopefully able to read all of them as we passed.

At noon, I remember stopping along the roadside, not certain what town we were near but we all enjoyed getting out of the car, having the picnic lunch mom had planned. I know on one such trip, mom happened to have a box of chocolate covered cherries which she kept in the glove compartment. Whenever us kids got restless, and that seemed pretty often, she would ration out a candy to each of us. It kept us content for a while but didn't keep us from asking the infamous question, "Are we there yet?"

When we finally got to Kimball and got to grandma's house, it was so exciting to be there and to see everyone. Almost immediately, Uncle Frank had us kids go with him to the horse tank, he took out a couple of bottles of home made root beer. It was quite cool as the windmill was pumping cool water into the tank. This was a great treat. I think Uncle Frank got as much enjoyment out of watching us drink it as he did making it.

Grandma was a jolly, happy lady, enjoyed cooking. We always had great meals, and the ever present kolaches. The country seemed to be overrun with jack rabbits and several times, the uncles Frank, Joe, John, and dad would go out at night to hunt them. The men would ride on the hood of the car and running boards watching for rabbits as the bright lights of the car picked them up. I think Gary may have gotten to go along and ride inside the car. There were always plenty of rabbits for stew.

Grandma Valasek, Aunt Emma Vodehnal and her young son, Donnie.

One time when we were there, it seems like Aunt Emma and Cousin Donnie were also there. We were having a big dinner and a number of pies were made. Everyone was commenting on how good they all looked. I remember sitting by Aunt Nellie and saying I wanted to be sure I got a certain piece of pie. She

Uncle John, Mom, Grandma
Valasek, Aunt Emma and
Uncle Joe. In front, Gary,
Alyce and Cousin Donnie.

Dad on the right
with friend Charlie Flakus
after a rabbit hunt
in Kimball.

The Kimball relatives,
Grandma Valasek, her sons,
Frank, John, Sr. and Joe.
Little boys in front, Leonard
and John, John Srs. sons.

immediately stuck my thumb in it and said it was mine. She and Uncle John always enjoyed laughing, having fun. Through the years, I've often wished that all families could live such a fun-loving, joyful life.

Uncle John, Aunt Nellie Valasek.

Chapter 14

...remembering Christmas!

The angel said to them: "You have nothing to fear!
I come to proclaim good news to you - tidings of great joy
to be shared by the whole people. This day in David's city
a savior has been born to you, the Messiah and Lord."
~Luke 2:10-11

I still remember the thrill when the Sears Christmas catalogue came in the mail. What an exciting time. Gary and I would literally devour every page, thrilled looking at all the lovely holiday clothes but especially the toy section. Most importantly, I spent hours dreaming over the 'baby doll section". There were cuddly, cozy little dolls with lovely clothes, fancy little dresses, pretty coats with little fur collars and tiny little shoes.

I knew that I probably could not have one but I still remember the dream of having one of those special dolls.

One Christmas I received a wonderful set of new flannel doll clothes. There was a little white petticoat with eyelet edging along the hem and a little flower embroidered on the bodice. There was a light blue dress, a pink coat and bonnet. Excitedly, there was also one-piece pajamas, in a Popeye print. I think the excitement was because mom had made me a one-piece pajama also in the same Popeye print. I was small and it didn't occur to me that mom had made the doll clothes, I just thought Santa was clever to give me the little doll pajamas in the same print as I had. The clothes fit my old baby doll perfectly. The dreams of a new doll vanished. There may be a lesson there. *In this prosperous age, we feel a need to give our children exactly what they ask for when improvising in a special effort as my mother did during difficult times, may be the wiser gift to our children.*

There was one Christmas I wanted a toy typewriter. It looked so exciting in the Sears Catalogue. I was so surprised to receive a little one that had a circle dial on it with the alphabet and numbers on it. I could turn the circle to the letter or number I wanted, press a bar and it would print one letter or number. With patience I could type a lot of words. That really was a fun toy. Usually we didn't get gifts out of the catalogue. Mom and Dad would make our toys or clothes.

One Christmas eve when we were unable to go to church because of the cold weather. We sat around the heater in the living room eating nuts. We were lucky to have an assortment of

Brazil nuts, walnuts, almonds, peanuts. We thought it was great fun to shell the nuts and eat them because this was the only time of the year we had them. I remember we also had oranges and apples. It really seemed like a wonderful evening, the memory still lingers. The only gift I recall receiving that Christmas was a little black Scotty dog bank. It had a little red bow around its neck. Undoubtedly there may have been a few more gifts, but probably not many. It was a time when there simply wasn't much money to purchase anything but bare necessities. That pretty little bank must have made an impression on me, realizing that it was a gift mom and dad made a special effort to get. The little bank sits on my printer now as I am writing. It is strange how the present time connects with the past.

I enjoyed coloring pictures. I don't recall having crayons until I started grade school. I do remember being enchanted with receiving a set of colors (crayons) for Christmas and being able to make pretty pictures. Sometimes I would also get a coloring book. I remember having one about Andy Hardy (Mickey Rooney). There was something endearing, enticing about this seemingly small person involved with his many antics.

Another time I got a coloring book that had pictures for every day of the week. 'This is the way we wash our clothes early Monday morning' or 'This is the way we iron our clothes every Tuesday morning'; or 'This is the way we mend our clothes early Wednesday morning'; 'This is the way we go to market early Thursday morning'; 'This is the way we clean our house early Friday morning'; 'This is the way we do our baking early Saturday morning'; and finally, 'This is the way we go to church so early Sunday morning'. I remember how carefully I selected my colors and how carefully I colored the pictures. I was fascinated by the pictures of the women doing their house chores, things that a little girl would dream doing someday. Each day had a special chore. I wonder, do they still print this type of coloring book?

Another time that really thrilled me was a gift from my Aunt Julie, Uncle Paul and Grandpa Pete. We were at their farm home south west of Loup City one Christmas day. The coloring book was one of those big ones, about two inches thick. I had never seen so large a coloring book filled with all kinds of pictures, trees, flowers, people, children. I thought it was the most exciting gift. I loved to draw and color and still remember how carefully I labored over every picture to color it 'just right'.

One year we were at my grandma Valasek's home in Kimball for Christmas. Gary and I each received a large set of water color paints. It was a black tin box about eight by ten inches in size. My big box had many little trays of dozens of colors. I had never had anything so beautiful, or knew there were so many shades of every color. I think that was the year we went to visit my Uncle John and Aunt Nellie Valasek at their farm south of Kimball. I still remember mom and Aunt Nellie having us kids look out a window and see 'Santa's footprints' in the snow and sure enough, later on we heard him making a noise on the roof top. I don't remember any gifts, but I do remember the excitement of Santa coming.

Christmas at school was met with great anticipation by all the students and the teacher. We always made a little gift for our parents. One year the teacher helped draw a design for a little teapot on some thin wood. She helped me saw it out and then paint it a bright red. We put a bright colored decal on the front of it, and two little hooks on the front of it and it became a hot pad holder. Mom seemed very pleased with it, she kept it hanging in her kitchen all her life. I now have it hanging over the stove in my kitchen, cherishing the memory of so very long ago. I vaguely remember Gary making a wooden shoe rack for dad. It had a couple of round dowels between two curved end pieces so it would hold two shoes. It seems like he painted it blue. I remember dad seemed pleased with this gift, also. One year the teacher showed the students how to paint bright colored pictures or flowers on a little square of clear glass. Usually the picture was outlined in black, giving it a stained glass look. Making gifts was a new experience for us and we thought we had made some very clever items.

Christmas at school was also a time for the big annual program. All children were included in some portion of the program. It might be in a Christmas play, sing a solo, duet or an all-school chorus. Most of us were enchanted by the expectation of the special holiday. We would help set up the Christmas tree, bring gifts for the teacher and one of the students. Most of the students helped make paper chains out of red and green construction paper to decorate the tree. I believe the teacher brought strings of popcorn. I don't recall if there were Christmas balls or lights but I do remember the excitement of a big decorated tree at the front of the class room. We all knew that Santa would be coming after the program. All of us small students were so excited, so eager to see Santa even though we were a bit frightened by him. In those days, Santa always seemed to wear a mask and some kind of beard. As a small child I would wonder about being able to see a face behind the mask but it didn't keep me from accepting a gift he might hand me. I know I refused to sit on his lap. It was a great thrill to receive a little bag of candy that contained the characteristic ribbon candy, something we don't see much today.

Chapter 15

...remembering Easter!

The people who walked in darkness
have seen a great light:
Upon those who dwelt in the land of gloom,
a light has shone.
~Isaiah 9:1

As a child, I recall Easter as being an exciting holiday, close to the excitement I felt at Christmas. It was routine for us kids to build 'nests' of straw in the yard, ready for the Easter bunny to find. In my child's mind, I still remember how I would imagine the big white Easter bunny in his bright colored clothes, hopping around.

It was such a thrill to hurry out on Easter morning and find the goodies. Usually there would always be a few colored hard cooked eggs. At that time, we kids had never seen or helped to dye eggs so it was a great treat to find these eggs in the nest. There might also be a few jelly beans and the traditional bright colored Easter candies, sort of a formed sugar center with a hard candy shell coating. Candy was a treat so anything we got was a wonderful treat.

Then there was the time, when I was a bit older, I had gotten up early and as I looked out the north bedroom window, I saw the Easter bunny placing some goodies in a row in the garden. I always seemed to be a sensitive child and I never told my mother that I saw the bunny.

There aren't a lot memories about Easter, but I do remember being at Grandpa Peter's farm for Easter dinner one time and Aunt Julie had gotten each of us kids one of those medium sized chocolate bunnies, decorated with bright colored frosting flowers. It was so pretty, I didn't eat it for several days. I just wanted to look at it.

Of course the important part of Easter was getting dressed and going to Mass (church) in Sargent. Most people didn't buy new clothes very often. If families were able to buy something new, it seemed that they bought them at Easter time. It was exciting to have a new dress, maybe a new hat or bonnet, maybe new, shoes and stockings. Little girls often wore little white gloves and had a tiny white pocket book. People generally took notice of each other, seeing what new apparel others might have. One time my great aunt Sophie Visek gave me a small bright green purse with a little handle. The important thing was that it had shiny copper penny glued to the outside of it as a decoration. I surely thought it was the most fabulous gift. I cherished that little purse. It must have touched me deeply, that I have been able to recall having it after all these years.

Chapter 16

...Mom's Favorite Recipes

He took the seven loaves and the fish,
and after giving thanks he broke them
and gave them to the disciples,
who in turn gave them to the crowds.
~Matthew 15:36

Mom may have been best known for setting a bountiful table. Relatives, friends and neighbors recall the many wonderful meals she served. There always seemed to be fresh baked bread, kolaches, pies and full course meals. In those days, a good cook, certainly a Czech cook always set a table full of delicious, mouth watering dishes. Always a big platter of meat, mashed potatoes, creamy gravy, two or three vegetables, relishes, fresh baked bread, rolls (rolichi, kolaches, biscuits), fresh churned butter. The meal always ended with fresh baked fruit pies or a frosted cake. She had a habit of urging her guests to take more, eat more. She loved watching people 'enjoy' her cooking.

She was a shy, retiring lady, never quite comfortable in speaking up, or voicing her opinion, even when she may have had better ideas

*Special dishes used
for company.*

then those around her. She was always afraid of hurting someone's feelings. She wanted people to be comfortable in her home.

KOLACHES
Grandma Valasek's Kolache Dough
1 can Evaporated Milk (2 cups)   ½ cup shortening
½ cup sugar   1 teaspoon salt
Heat milk, dissolve the shortening, sugar and salt in the milk.
Beat 2 eggs and add to cooled mixture.
Dissolve 1 package yeast in ¼ cup warm water & 1 teaspoon sugar.
5 cups flour, alternate milk & yeast mixtures. Should be a soft but firm dough.

Kolache Technique
Take large spoonful of dough, roll in hands to make smooth ball, place on greased cookie sheet. Continue until cookie sheet is filled evenly, leave space between dough balls. Lightly butter tops of balls. Using the three middle fingers of each hand, make a well defined dent in each ball, cover and let rise. When dough is about double, again make well defined dents in each dough ball. Add desired filling, apricot, cherry, prune, cottage cheese, etc. The crumb topping can be sprinkled on the fruit filling during the last 8 to 10 minutes baking time.

Cottage Cheese/Cream Cheese Filling
Amounts depend on number of kolaches you plan to bake. Proportions listed are for 12 ounces of drained cottage cheese.
Cream Cheese, 4 ounces soften
Egg yolk, 1 lightly beaten
Sugar, 1/3 cup or to taste
Raisins, 1/3 cup or as desired
Tapioca, 1 tablespoon

Stir ingredients together. It is important to sweeten this mixture for the best flavor. Very good!

Prune or Apricot Filling
Cook 1 cup till very tender, remove pits. Add sugar, can make it quite sweet. Add ½ teaspoon lemon juice. Don't make to stiff or runny.

Kolache Crumb Topping (a favorite of mom)
1/3 cup sugar
3/4 cup flour
1/3 cup butter

Mix together to form small crumbs. Sprinkle on kolaches' about five minutes before they are done baking.

Fried Bread
Use roll dough or bread dough. Mom generally used bread dough. Heat oil in large pan till a small piece of dough browns in a few seconds.
Measure off large tablespoons of dough. May need to dust lightly so it doesn't stick. Stretch between your fingers until center is very thin, with the edges a bit thicker. Don't worry about shape. Fry two or three at a time, don't crowd pan. Watch closely and turn soon as bottoms are golden brown. Finish bottom side, drain excess oil, dip immediately in a bowl of sugar. Eat with coffee or milk. Very good!

Crock with lid,
used countless times
for bread dough
to rise.

Pineapple Dessert
This must have been a favorite of mom's. I found at least 6 recipes in one book.

18 graham crackers (crushed)

1 cup milk, heat to boiling point
26 large marshmallows, melt in milk, let cool

1 cup seasoned whipped cream with 1 small can crushed   pineapple (drained) added

Stir milk, marshmallow, whipped cream and pineapples together. Line 9"x13" pan with ½ the graham crackers. Spread mixture on evenly. Top with remaining crackers. *(This is a simple, tasty dessert. Mom used to like making it for us kids.)*

Rhubarb Cake

1/2 cup shortening   1 1/2 cup sugar
1/2 teaspoon salt, cream together.
1 egg, continue mix together.
1 cup sour milk
1 teaspoon soda, mix milk and soda together.
2 cups + 1 tablespoon flour.

Alternate flour, milk with above mixture.

3 cups rhubarb, diced, add to mixture. Spread mixture in 9"x13" greased pan.

Topping: 1/3 cup sugar, 1/3 cup chopped nuts, 1 teaspoon cinnamon, mix and sprinkle over unbaked cake. Bake at 350 degrees, 45 minutes or until knife comes out clean. Very good!

Ice Box Rolls

2 cups water
1/2 cup sugar
2 tablespoons butter
1 tablespoon salt, mix together 1st four ingredients, boil this and let cool.

Add 2 beaten eggs and 4 cups flour to above mixture, mix well. Dissolve 2 yeast cakes in ¼ cup warm water and 1 teaspoon sugar. Add to above mixture. Add 4 more cups flour (use your judgment). Mix down, put in cool place or refrigerate overnight. *Comment by mom - good!*

A simple dish, almost always used to hold mashed potatoes, and now it holds so many memories.

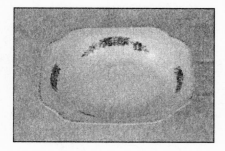

Ice Box Rolls *(another version)*

1 cup scalded milk	1/2 cup fat
1/2 cup sugar	2 eggs
1 cake fresh yeast	1/2 cup warm water
1/2 cup mashed potatoes	1 teaspoon salt
Flour	

This is the way many recipes were handed around, lady to lady. The ingredients were listed, expectation was that the women knew how to put the ingredients together.

Cinnamon Rolls (Czech technique)

Take balls of dough, roll in hands to make a narrow 'dough' rope. Dip in bowl of cream or ½ & ½, then a sugar/cinnamon mixture, gently roll rope into a cinnamon roll, place in buttered 9"x13" pan. Continue till pan is full. Rolls may touch but don't overfill pan. For a 'gooey-er roll' you can spread brown sugar, drizzle some flavored syrup (maple) or honey and some chopped nuts in the bottom of pan before you add the rolls. Immediately after baking, turn pan over so rolls come out easily.

Yeast Starter *(Here's an oldie!)*

1/2 cup sugar	1/2 cup flour
1/2 teaspoon salt	4 cups mashed potatoes

Beat together. Add 1 pint potato water. Add 1/2 cake yeast soaked in 1/2 cup warm water. Let set in warm place 24 hours. When ready to bake bread, use 1 cup starter, add to this 1 cup water, 1 tablespoon lard, 1 tablespoon sugar and salt to taste.
Set this thin sponge in the morning and let it get light, then add flour to make dough as usual.

Pickled Pigs Feet

Clean pigs feet. Place in stone jar, cover with brine made by dissolving two pounds of pure salt in one gallon water. Let stand 10 days. Remove from brine and soak in cold water 3 to 4 hours. Drop feet into hot water and cook slowly until tender (not until bones separate from flesh). Pack in hot jars, cover with boiling spiced vinegar. (Use ½ gallon vinegar, 2 tablespoons horseradish, 1 bay leaf, 1 small red pepper pod, 1 teaspoon black peppercorns, 1 teaspoon whole allspice).

Creamed Cabbage

Shred cabbage, cook till just tender in lightly salted water. Drain. Add ½ cup cream, 1 teaspoon caraway seed, a dash of pepper. Can add a bit of sugar to enhance flavor.

Four Layer Dessert

1st layer:
1 cup flour
1/2 cup margarine, melted
1/2 cup pecans, chopped

Combine ingredients and pat into 9"x13" pan. Bake 15 minutes in 350 degree oven. Cool completely.

2nd layer:
8 ounce cream cheese, softened
1 cup powdered sugar
1 cup cool whip

Mix all together and spread on top of 1st layer. Chill thoroughly again.

3rd layer:
2 pkgs. Instant pudding mix (any flavor)
3 cups milk
1 teaspoon vanilla

Simple utensils and platter, a mainstay of the farm kitchen.

Mix and beat till thick, pour over previous layers, chill well again.

4th layer:
Top with additional cool whip and sprinkle with chopped pecans.
Cool again. *This was Aunt Cookie's Recipe (Lucille Synak) Very good!*

Rhubarb Meringue Pie
1 cup diced rhubarb
1 cup sugar
2 eggs
1 cup milk
1/8 teaspoon nutmeg
2 tablespoons flour

Mix sugar, milk, egg yolks, flour & nutmeg together. Pour over rhubarb in unbaked pie shell. Bake till almost done, knife comes out clean. Top with meringue and brown.

Corn Bread

3/4 cup corn meal
1 tablespoon shortening
1 egg
¼ cup sugar
4 teaspoons baking powder

1 1/4 cup flour
1/2 teaspoon salt
1 cup milk

Mix together, bake at 425 degrees for 25 minutes. (This was grandma Valasek's recipe)

Spicy Oven Fried Chicken

2 to 3 ½ # fryer
½ cup buttermilk
Marinade a couple hours or overnight.

½ cup cornmeal
1 ½ teaspoon salt
1 ½ teaspoon chili or paprika
½ teaspoon oregano, crushed

1/2 cup flour

1/4 teaspoon pepper

Drain chicken, dip in above dry mixture. Place pieces in large baking pan, skin side up. Drizzle with 1/3 cup melted butter or margarine. Bake 375 degrees about 50 minutes or till done.

Cranberry-Apple Salad

2 cups uncooked cranberries
1 large red apple, diced
1 cup celery, chopped
1/2 cup walnuts, chopped
1 1/2 cup sugar

Grind cranberries, mix with above ingredients and let set till juice forms. Dissolve 1 package lemon Jell-O in 1 ½ cup hot water. Let set till cool, add cranberry mixture and let set. *(This was a favorite of mom's for Thanksgiving and Christmas dinners. Very good.)*

Dinner Salad

1/2 cup cheese, American diced
1/2 cup celery, diced
1/2 cup pineapple tidbits, drained
1/2 cup walnuts, coarsely chopped
1 package Jell-O, dissolve in 2 cups hot water, cool.
1 package Dream Whip, whip stiffly then fold into cooled Jell-O.

Add first four ingredients and chill. *(I called this the ½ & ½ salad, it is easy to remember the ingredients.)*

Gravy dish, rarely used for anything else.

Porcupine Meatballs

1# ground beef
1/2 cup regular rice
1/2 cup water
1/3 cup chopped onion
1 teaspoon salt
1/2 teaspoon celery salt
1/8 teaspoon garlic powder
1/8 teaspoon pepper

Mix, shape into balls and brown on all sides in 2 tablespoons fat.
Tasty Gravy:
1 can (15 ounce) tomato sauce
2 teaspoon Worcestershire sauce
1 cup water

Stir and pour over meatballs in a heavy skillet. Cover and simmer on low heat about 45 minutes. Add a bit more water if needed. Serves 4 to 6.

Jeternice or Iternice (Bohemian Liver Sausage)
Boil a pigs head in salted water (if too fat, trim it off). Boil until tender. Take meat off bone and grind. Save the liquid for the bread. Take about half of the liver and put in boiling water, let set a few minutes just enough to set the blood, then grind. Soak bread in the liquid and squeeze dry. Mix meats together, use one part ground meat to one and a half parts dry bread. (old bread is best). Season to taste with salt, pepper, a few garlic cloves (mashed to paste). Fry a little in a skillet to check taste, if more seasoning is needed. Add additional liquid so mixture is soft but not runny. If you are planning to fill casings, they can be purchased at any meat market. Stuff and tie into links. Put sausages a few at a time in hot water and simmer. (Rapid boiling may burst them). When they rise to the top, take out and put in cold water for a few minutes to cool. Remove from water and lay on towels to cool. Now they are ready to eat or freeze.
If you don't want to use casings, the sausage may be put in small freezer containers. When needed, thaw slightly and fry in a lightly greased skillet till crusty. Very good.

Jelita (Bohemian Blood Sausage)
For the Jelita, save some of the liver sausage and add minced onion fried in lard, some barley boiled in salted water and cooled. Add enough blood to make it juicy but not runny. Season to taste. Fry a little in a skillet to check taste, need for more seasoning. Fill casings and boil like the liver sausage, or place in freezer containers for later use. Seasonings depend on the amount of meat, you need to check for your own preference

Sultz (Pickled Pork Hocks)
Pork Hocks, split on sides	2 grains whole Allspice
2 to 3 quarts of Water	Pepper
2 tablespoons Salt	Vinegar
1 Onion, diced	

Boil hocks in water with the salt, onion and allspice until very tender. Cook, debone and dice. Strain broth and add plenty of pepper and vinegar. They lose their strength in the cooling process. Ass diced meat and heart just long enough to heart through. Pour into a deep crock and set aside to congeal, usually overnight. Meat must be covered by the broth. Slice and serve cold. Wonderful with fresh baked bread. Usually a light sprinkle of vinegar over the slices enhances the flavor. Tip: Other cuts of pork may be added to the hocks.

Convertible Broccoli & Chicken Casserole
Convertible because it can be prepared with the chicken breasts and broccoli spears for company dinner or you can use chopped broccoli and diced dark and light chicken for a family meal.
2 boxes frozen broccoli spears (or chopped)
21/2 cans Cream of Chicken soup
6 whole chicken breasts or (4 cups diced chicken)
1 ¼ cup mayonnaise
1 teaspoon lemon juice
¾ cup grated cheddar cheese
¾ cup buttered bread crumbs

Partially cook broccoli, drain well.
Stew chicken until tender.

Place broccoli into lightly buttered 9"x13" baking pan
Place chicken over top of broccoli, lightly season with celery & onion salt. Combine soup, lemon juice and mayonnaise, pour over top of broccoli & chicken mixture. Spread cheddar cheese over mixture. Top with bread crumbs. Bake 1 hour until lightly browned, 350°

Although this recipe was made many years after I had left home, I had won 1ˢᵗ place in the North Platte Telegraph recipe contest in 1981. Mom was so proud of this, so decided to include it in the book. I had modified the recipe handed down to me from Aunt Nellie Valasek.

Cheese Melt
2# Velveeta cheese
2# Imitation cheese
8 ounces extra sharp cheese
4 1/2 cans evaporated milk
1 tablespoon Caraway Seed (optional)

In upper double boiler pan, cut up cheese, place over boiling water
and beat until melted and smooth. Store in jars, may seal with wax.

DILL SOUP, A Czech Delight
Potatoes, 2 medium diced in small pieces.
Dill leaves, fresh if possible, or dry weed.
If fresh, I snip at least 2 tblsp. If dry, 1 tbsp or to your taste. You
want a good dill flavor. Add enough water to cover potatoes. Season
to taste with salt. Cover, cook till just tender. **Do not drain.**

Buttermilk, 1 quart
Flour, 2 tablespoons

Mix flour with buttermilk, beat until smooth.
Slowly pour mixture into potato mixture.
Sour Cream, 8 oz., add to milk and potatoes, bring to slow boil.
Eggs, 2 to 3 per person.
Break eggs carefully into mixture, being careful not to break yolks.
Allow to simmer slowly about 10 to 12 minutes until yolks are firm. If
you stir, do it gently so as not to disturb egg content.
Season to taste with salt and pepper (white or black).
You can garnish with a sprig of dill or dry dill weed.
Serve with thick slices of bread, rye, French, etc.

NOTE: You may be tempted to add onion. **DON'T.**
You don't want to cover the dill flavor.
*If you don't care for the buttermilk flavor, you can use
whole or 2% milk, thicken as noted above. Use the sour
cream. In late summer when there are new potatoes and fresh dill,
this is especially tasty.*

TIP: I spray the pot with PAM before I start the potatoes.
It seems to keep the milk mixture from sticking. Also, just recently I
found that if I poach the eggs till slightly set, then add them to the milk
mixture, they hold their shape nicely.

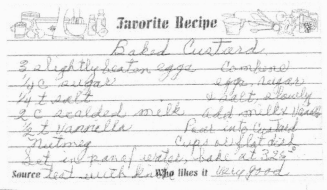

Favorite Recipe

Baked Custard

3 slightly beaten eggs — Combine
1/2 c sugar — egg, sugar
1/4 t salt — & salt, slowly
2 c scalded milk — add milk & vanilla
1/2 t vanilla — Pour into Custard
Nutmeg — cups or flat dish
Set in pan of water, bake at 325°

Source _Test with knife_   Who likes it _very good_

In Bohemian: Prize Winning Apple Strudel Recipe
(See next page for American version)

Tageny Strudl z Jablek
Vlej to mísi 1/4 kořlěku vlažného,
mléka, a rozpusť v něm kousek
másla (asi jako půl vejce.) Přidej
k tomu celé vejce, 1/4 kořlěku cukru
a trošek soli, asi hvat mouky a
zadělej na tuhý těsto. Jako na nuktích
vysyp na val, a válečkem dobře uhněť
Přeloz miskou a nech hodinu odpočinout
Pak si připrav nastrouhne jabka, Pak
umaž na másle Chleba (Bread
crumbs) Ja va teť chleba nedávam
kovám cornflakes povitaky dobre
    Pak prostři ze na stůl a
poczp troschu mouchou a vital-
ný těsto tenaunce, po něm dej
jabka, rozinki a smazeny chleba
cukrem a skorici a pokrop rozpuste-
ným máslem, a trochu smetanou
Pak strudl sviň a pomaž máslem
a peč asi hodinu dis je na půl
pečeny tak ze podlyej mlekem a
kořlěk a necha se do peci.

Apple Strudl Prize Winning Recipe

Take 2 cups white flour, work in ½ cup butter, add ¼ teasp salt, & ¼ cup sugar add 2 well beaten eggs add 1 cup milk, then add enough flour to make dough as stiff as for noodles, let rest before rolling, roll out to ⅛ in thick or pull it. then fry bread crumbs in butter, add apples, sugar, (I sprinkled poppy seed ground) ½ cup walnuts, 1 cup coconut, wet edge in water, roll up. Put in pan, brush with butter, while it bakes brush with cream or milk every 15 mins. Bake in moderate oven 1 hr.

Anna's Memos:

Found in mom's note book.

Mondays child is fair of face.
Tuesdays child is full of grace.
Wednesdays child is free from woe.
Thursdays child is delightful to know.
Fridays child is loving and caring.
Saturdays child is kind and sharing.
Sundays child brings joy from the start.
Each child is special and dear to the heart.

EPILOGUE

Do not neglect the gift that is in you.
1 Timothy 4:14

As I end this book of memories, I mostly wanted to remember the loving care my dad and mother managed to give Gary and me during very poor, difficult years, years of hardship. The greatest gift they gave us was their love for each of us. That love continued through the generations to their nine grandchildren, and on to the great grandchildren. They were so proud of my daughter Rachael, and each of Gary's five sons, Patrick, Gregory, Kevin, Mark, William and three daughters, Denise, Coleen, and Jodi.

Their legacy lives on now in how well we live and love and carry on their caring tradition through our children and our grandchildren.

ALYCE AND GARY
GROWING UP

Ready for 4-H Show in Broken Bow. Alyce with her Angus steer 'Toby' and Gary with his Angus steer 'Jeep'.

Alyces' graduation picture St. Francis School of Nursing, Grand Island, Nebraska.

Cpl. Gerald J. Zulkoski, served in Pusan, Korea.

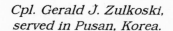

Index Reference to persons mentioned or pictured in the book.

Zulkoski, William (123)

Zulkoski, Sylvester (Sal) (58);

Zulkoski, Peter (Foreword, Wedding picture, 58, 59, 98, 102)

Zulkoski, Paul (59, 98)

Zulkoski, Patrick (123)

Zulkoski, Michael (Mike) (27, 59)

Zulkoski, Marthann (59)

Zulkoski, Mark (123)

Zulkoski, Kevin (123)

Zulkoski, Julia (59, 63, 98, 102)

Zulkoski, Gregory (123)

Zulkoski, Gerald (Gary) (Copyright pg., Acknowledgments, Foreword, Picture pgs., 3, 4, 5, 7, 23, 25, 26, 27, 41, 45, 50, 53, 55, 58, 59, 62, 63, 64, 65, 66, 69, 70, 74, 84, 85, 86, 93, 95, 98, 99, 123, 125, 126)

Zulkoski, Floyd (Foreword)

Zulkoski, Casimir (dad) (Copyright pg., Dedication, Foreword, Picture pgs.1, 2, 3, 8, 9, 18, 19, 41, 44, 45, 46, 47, 51, 58, 59, 65, 67, 69, 70, 76, 77, 78, 79, 81, 84, 85, 86, 92, 93, 99, 123)

Zulkoski, Anthony (Foreword)

Zulkoski, Anna Michalski (Foreword, Wedding picture)

Zulkoski, Anna (mom) (Copyright pg., Dedication, Foreword, Picture pgs.2, 3, 5, 6, 8, 9, 10, 12, 13, 14, 17, 18, 19, 23, 30, 41, 42, 43, 47, 48, 54, 58, 59, 63, 68, 73, 76, 77, 78, 79, 80, 81, 84, 85, 86, 87, 88, 90, 91, 93, 99, 104, 121, 123)

Zulkoski, Alyce (Copyright pg., Foreword, Picture pgs.26, 45. 58. 59, 63, 64, 93, 125, 126)

Wescott, Gibbon & Braggs Store (17, 21))

Wenburg, Jodi (Zulkoski) (123)

Weekly, Harry E. (35, 36)

Vodehnal, Emma (56, 57, 92, 93),

Vodehnal, Donald (Donnie) (56, 57, 63, 64, 92, 93)

Vodehnal, Bill (56, 57)

Visek, Vencil (75)

Visek, Sophie (75, 102)

Visek, Mary (60, 61)

Visek, Marilee (60, 63, 64)

Visek, Joseph (60, 63, 64)

Visek, Joe (60, 61)

Visek, Jim (75)

Visek, Irene (32, 75)
Visek, Ilene (32, 75)
Visek, Evelyn (21, 31)
Visek, Betty Ann (60, 63, 64)
Valasek, Nellie (62, 94, 98, 115)
Valasek, Leonard (62, 64, 93)
Valasek, John, Jr. (62, 64, 93)
Valasek, John (62, 92, 93, 94, 98)
Valasek, Joe (90, 92, 93)
Valasek, Frank (uncle) (90, 91, 92, 93)
Valasek, Frank (Foreword pg.)
Valasek, Emma Ptacnik (Foreword pg., 9, 79, 90, 91, 92, 93, 105)
Thurman, Gerald A. (37, 38, 39, 40)
Szczesny, Father Michael (73)
Synak, Lucille (Cookie) (59)
Student List, Longwood School 1937-1946 (Pages 35, 36, 37, 38, 39, 40)
Smith, Charles (59)
Smith, Anne (59)
Siudowski, Father Thomas (74)
Sister Fabian (72)
Sister Borgia (72)
Simpson, Eva (12)
Shanks, Arline (40)
Rea, Margaret (55)
Plock, Vera (38)
Pester, Margaret (38)
Pearl, Shirley (Foreword)
O'Neill, Denise (Zulkoski) (123)
Olson, Martha (38)
Old 101 Writers Group, Acknowledgments
Ochsner, Olga (18, 19)
Ochsner, LeAnn (20)
Ochsner, John Dean (20)
Ochsner, John (18, 19)
Ochsner, Danny (20)
Moser, Rachael (Zulkoski) (123)
Moreau, Andrea (Copyright pg., Acknowledgments)
Milton, Ann (Copyright pg., Acknowledgments)
McGrew, Dr. Kirby (Foreword)
Lukesh, Mary (20)
Lukesh Creamery & Ice Cream Parlor (20)

Lewin, Wayne (12, 13, 46)
Lewin, June (12, 13,)
Lenstrom, Ruth (39)
Lebruska's Shoe Repair Shop (15)
Kokes, Freda (39)
Hugo, Stella (83)
Hugo, Herbie (83)
Hugo, Harry (82, 83)
Hlavinka, George (38)
Gilmore, Mary (40)
Gawrick family (74, 74)
Fricke Blacksmith Shop (15)
Flakus, Charlie (93)
Chalupsky's (27)
Chalupa, Rosie Brim (24, 35, 36, 37)
Burgess, Coleen (Zulkoski) (123)
Blackledge, Keith (Copyright pg., Acknowledgments pg.)
Billie Joe (17)
Berger, Father Bernard (Practice of Virtues pg.)

. . .ABOUT
THE
AUTHOR

She laughingly says it took her eight years to get through nurses training. After one year at St. Joseph's School Nursing, Omaha, she quit until graduating as a registered nurse from St. Francis School of Nursing, Grand Island eight years later. She cherishes her classes at Duschesne College and Creighton University, Omaha.

Alyce attained her Bachelor's and Master's Degree in Education at Kearney State College while working full-time at Great Plains Regional Medical Center in North Platte, Nebraska.

Most of her working career has been in the hospitals in North Platte. The last fifteen years were as education director, later as Continuing Medical Education and Community Health Coordinator.

In 1993, she received the Woman of Achievement Award in Education from the North Platte Chamber of Commerce Community Improvement Committee.

Her love of art and writing was put on hold while she worked full-time, but the dream to pursue writing her story was always hovering. Alyce says she is hopeful that as people read her story, they will realize the importance of their own stories, share them with their families, preserve those memories, the heritage that is theirs.

Order Form
for additional copies of

FOREVER SPRING
by Alyce Zulkoski

Telephone Orders: 308-532-7232

Email Orders Alyceaz@nponline.com

Postal Orders: Alyce Zulkoski
                 1307 Burlington
                 North Platte, NE 69101

Please send _____ copies of Forever Spring @ $12.95 each plus $4.00 shipping and handling.

Total Enclosed: _____

Name: _____

Address: _____

City, State, ZIP: _____

Thank You
for
your order!